PARSIFAL
THE WILL AND REDEMPTION

"Exploring Richard Wagner's Final Treatise"

by John L. Mastrogiovanni, D.Min.

Copyright © 2014
Revised Edition 2.0

"EXPLORING RICHARD WAGNER'S FINAL TREATISE"

Copyright © 2014
John L. Mastrogiovanni, D.Min.

All rights reserved. No part of this book may be reproduced in any form without written permission from the author, except for brief quotations in a review or lecture.

Wagner's letter quotations were referenced from Selected Letters of Richard Wagner Barry Millington, J.M. Dent & Sons LTD Copyright © 1987 Used by permission

Scripture quotations taken from the Amplified® Bible
Copyright © 1954, 1958, 1962, 1964, 1965, 1987 by The Lockman Foundation
Used by permission. (www.Lockman.org)

Scripture quotations taken from the New American Standard Bible®
Copyright © 1960, 1962, 1963, 1968, 1971, 1972, 1973
1975, 1977, 1995 by The Lockman Foundation
Used by permission. (www.Lockman.org)

Scripture taken from the New King James Version.
Copyright © 1982 by Thomas Nelson, Inc.
Used by permission. All rights reserved.

Scripture quotations marked NLT are taken from the Holy Bible, New Living Translation, copyright 1996, 2004. Used by permission of Tyndale House Publishers, Inc., Wheaton, Illinois 60189.
All rights reserved.

"PARSIFAL: THE WILL AND REDEMPTION"

TABLE OF CONTENTS

Acknowledgements .... - 5 -

Before the Curtain Rises .... - 7 -
VORSPIEL: Gesamtkunstwerk - Art Replaces Religion .- 25 -

ACT I .... - 37 -
PART 1: The Domain of Religion .... - 39 -
PART 2: Religion Threatened By Foolishness .... - 67 -
PART 3: Religion in the Inner World .... - 77 -

ACT II .... - 93 -
PART 1: The Obliviousness of Enlightenment .... - 95 -
PART 2: The Conflict of Reason and Divine Reality .... - 115 -
PART 3: Transformation and Reformation .... - 137 -

ACT III .... - 145 -
PART 1: The Prodigals Return .... - 147 -
PART 2: The Divine Revealed .... - 167 -

Walking Down the Green Hill .... - 189 -

Endnotes .... - 195 -

"EXPLORING RICHARD WAGNER'S FINAL TREATISE"

"PARSIFAL: THE WILL AND REDEMPTION"

Acknowledgements

I want to begin with my deepest and heartfelt thanks to my father, *John L. Mastrogiovanni, Sr.* who gave me one of the greatest gifts I've ever received; the introduction to the music of Richard Wagner at the age of five. From that time until now, a half century later, my love affair with Wagner's art has never waned. My life is all the richer on a daily basis for it... words cannot express!

My sincere gratitude to *the Late Dr. Sherwin Sloan,* former chairman of the Wagner Society of Southern California, who helped make a childhood dream come true fifteen years ago by making my first trip to Bayreuth possible.

A very special thank you to *Myriam Pommier,* former Festival blau Mädchen, who on my third trip to Bayreuth helped me when I was ill (me not speaking any conversational German) and aided in getting the medication I needed at the apotheke. I will never forget the conversation she and I had regarding Parsifal and Kundry's kiss.

A big thank you to Robert Torres, Bruce Bisenz, Paul Lowe, Eva Kirsch, and Nina Haro, my wonderful leadership team at the Wagner Society of Southern California. Without their help, being its new chairman in the shadow of Dr. Sloan would have been an almost impossible task, not to mention the continuing of his legacy with the wonderful Bayreuth Gala Dinners each year.

I would also like to thank Eva Wagner-Pasquier for her friendship, encouragement and kindness; it has been an inspiration. Her friendship is a treasure!

Last but not least, I want to thank my family: my wife Karen and my son Christopher, who have allowed all things Wagner to be in our living room, family room, car, home-office, even dining room! And also my married daughter (and fellow Wagnerian) Christina who has loved all things Wagner since the age of two when she used to say, "Put on the Hojotoho, Daddy!"

"EXPLORING RICHARD WAGNER'S FINAL TREATISE"

"PARSIFAL: THE WILL AND REDEMPTION"

Before the Curtain Rises

The brass choir decrescendos while the violins soar with the moving leitmotif of Redemption, originally titled the 'Glorification of Brünnhilde'. As the final chord sounds, we sit in awe as *Götterdämmerung* concludes. From stunned silence we slowly return to the domain of this world. We rise out of our armchair and approach our media system. As we remove the CD or DVD from the player, we're almost compelled to take the first disc of *Das Rheingold* to start the glorious cycle all over again. Then another thought dawns on us, do we dare reach for Wagner's next work to take us further on the ethereal journey? We just don't want the sublime music and enthralling experience to end. We want to stay in that special place between this realm and Heaven, the unearthly domain we call ... *Beyond* ...

According to Wagner that special realm beyond is called, *Redemption*. It's where humanity and the Divine[1] are clutched in united embrace. From *Holländer* to *Parsifal* (even in the earlier operas if one peers into them), Wagner takes us on that redemptive journey to worlds beyond ours. It's as if he cunningly grins at us, like a divine sorcerer, and in spite of whatever intellectual rationalizations we've made about politics, religion, faith, spirituality and the human condition, he persuades us past our own sentiments. Whether it's the music, the drama, or the poetic colors of the libretto, we willfully surrender. The craft of this sage is so potent it occurs without us realizing it. Even if we do, we succumb. His ideas are herald and we keep going back for more. As we pass our corporeal reasoning and resign belief, Wagner says:

> "Above all possibility of concrete thought, the Tone-poet Seer reveals to us the Inexpressible: we divine, no, feel! and see that this insistent World of the Will is also but a state that vanishes before the One: 'I know that my Redeemer liveth!'"[2]

> "One might say where Religion becomes artificial, it is reserved for Art to save the spirit of religion by recognizing the figurative values of the mythic symbols which the former would have us believe in their literal sense, and revealing their deep and hidden truth through an ideal presentation. ... But Religion has sunk into an artificial life, when she finds herself compelled to keep on adding to the edifice of her dogmatic symbols, and thus conceals the one divinely True in her beneath an ever growing heap of incredibilities commended to belief. Feeling this, she has always sought the aid of Art ..."[3]

Wagner wrote those words in his volume called, *Religion and Art*. He believed that where religion failed in its legalistic and concrete philosophical symbols, art had the power to transport the pilgrim to the door of experience and Divine presence. For Wagner, this idea of religion giving way to art was something that would be a consistent expression in his creativity throughout his life.

For young Wagner the merging of these worlds began at a critical time, when he was just six years old. His father, Friedrich Wagner, had died before his first birthday, and he had no memory of him. The only recollections were what his mother shared with him, which interestingly included a great love of the theater. Not shy of a year of his father's death, young Richard found his father's best friend, Ludwig Geyer, marrying his mother and taking on the role of stepfather. He was quite dedicated to young Richard's education and when he was of age he gave over his instruction to a minister friend just outside of Dresden.

Pastor Wetzel would give him his first, *"recollections of impressions of the world; in the evening the pastor would tell us of Robinson Crusoe, accompanied by instructive discussion. His reading aloud of a biography on Mozart made a great impression on me ..."*[4]. Just beyond that year of the tutelage of the good pastor, a letter was received for both Wetzel and young Richard to return to Dresden; Wagner's stepfather was dying. Upon arrival, the youth did not cope with the event well; it *"...came over me only as visions in a dream. ... My uneasy amazement was so great I was unable to cry."*[5] Within less than 24 hours, Ludwig was dead.

When we consider these important years, we find a fatherless boy impressed by the musical genius of Mozart, the lonely yet exciting adventures of Crusoe, all in the context of an influential man, a man of faith. What other lonely, fatherless boy do we know who was spurred on by adventure, who met a man of faith who helped him find his way, all framed by breathtaking music? Of course, *Parsifal*. You may add that this theme of fatherlessness, adventure and the interplay of redemption appears repetitively in Wagner's works; the two most obvious are Siegfried from *Der Ring Des Nibelungen*, and Parsifal from the opera that bears his name.

Mentioning Siegfried takes us back to the conclusion of *Götterdämmerung*. How does this pertain to *Parsifal?* According to Wagner in a letter written on August 11th 1873:

"I have felt compelled to use my Nibelung drama to build a Castle for the Grail devoted to art, far removed from the common ways of human activity: only there, in Monsalvat, can the longed for feat be revealed to the people ..."[6]

While in one respect Wagner is speaking of his opera house in Bayreuth, this connection goes far deeper. The operas themselves reveal their association. *Der Ring Des Nibelungen* is the material used to forge the foundation for *Parsifal*. It's as if to say, when Valhalla came burning down, in its place was found the Castle of the Grail. Thus, the pilgrims in *Der Ring Des Nibelungen* with its licentious dwarfs, broken gods and goddesses, and heroic Siegfried and Brünnhilde, emerge from Valhalla's ashes transfigured, completing their journey in the realm of Monsalvat. Siegfried, the fatherless, adventurous hero, is reincarnated as Parsifal, and Brünnhilde as Kundry. The connection of Kundry and her Valkyrie counterpart is made by Klingsor in the opening of the second act of *Parsifal*, when he proclaims:

KLINGSOR
Your Master calls you, nameless one, She-devil of old! Rose of Hell! Herodias you were - and what besides? Gundryggia there, Kundry here!

(Parsifal: Act II, Scene 1)

Gundryggia is an expansion of the old Scandinavian Valkyrie named Gundr (or Gunn), which means *battle-armor* or *protector*. The suffix Rygga is a past-tense verb meaning *traveled*. Ryggia is an extended Norwegian verb which also means *large fierce animal* from the root meaning, *fight* or *battle*. When put together, Gundryggia means *'Battle-Traveled-Protector'*; she was a serious force to be reckoned with. *Brünnhilde* is the same meaning and the German translation of Gundryggia, the lead warrior maiden and protector of Valhalla. The Valkyrie Gundryggia also rode a powerful horse and, in some cases, a huge wolf. The correlation of the symbology of a wolf and Valhalla is loosely associated in Act I of *Die Walküre* when Siegmund tells Hunding and Sieglinde his origins:

"PARSIFAL: THE WILL AND REDEMPTION"

> SIEGMUND
> "Wolf" was my father; I come into the world one of two, I and a twin sister. ... Warlike and strong was Wolf, enemies he gained plenty.
> *(Die Walküre: Act I, Scene 2)*

This analogy continues through the final scene of *Götterdämmerung* when Brünnhilde hurls herself on her horse Grane who was neighing eagerly to ride into the funeral pyre, to Act I of *Parsifal* when Kundry makes her entrance wildly riding a horse:

> 2nd SQUIRE
> See there, the wild rider!
>
> 1st SQUIRE
> Hey! How the mane of her devil's mare is flying!
>
> 2nd KNIGHT
> Ha! Is Kundry there?
>
> 1st KNIGHT
> She must be bringing momentous news!
>
> 2nd SQUIRE
> The mare is staggering.
>
> 1st SQUIRE
> Has she flown through the air?
>
> 2nd SQUIRE
> She is crawling over the ground.
> *(Parsifal: Act I, Scene 1)*

This will be the only time we'll witness her ride a horse; after her arrival it will be unnecessary for her to ride again. Thus, in *Götterdämmerung*, what Brünnhilde embodies rides off in its fiery conclusion, arriving in *Parsifal* transformed and reincarnated on a wild horse as Kundry.

Even the musicology affirms the connection and possibly gives us the clearest correlation. We find that the final note of the Redemption leitmotif in *Götterdämmerung*, played long and high on the violins, is an A^b. It's by no accident the *Parsifal* prelude begins with violins playing the Communion leitmotif also on A^b. For those who like studying such things, when using the aspect of music theory known as the Circle of Fifths,[7] as the violins play that same high A^b in *Götterdämmerung*, they do so in the key of D^b. If we locate the key of D^b in the Circle of Fifths, we also find that the next key in its progression is A^b. Needless to say, in what key does *Parsifal* begin? *A^b, of course!* The musical and dramatic connections between *Der Ring Des Nibelungen* and *Parsifal* are undeniable according to Wagner, both in word and artistic action.

But what of the philosophical connections? While we will not discuss the numerous spiritual and philosophical ramifications of the *Der Ring Des Nibelungen*, which would easily be a book in itself, we will reflect briefly here on how *Götterdämmerung* ends. Who is really redeemed? Surely not Alberich, though he continues to live on. Definitely not Hagan (Alberich's son), Siegfried's nemesis; he's drowned by the Rhinemaidens. The Gibichungs die as their hall burns because of Brünnhilde's immolation. The gods and heroes are cremated in Valhalla as it crashes and burns.

Brünnhilde, of course is the one who sacrifices herself to cleanse the effects of the cursed ring; most definitely this is a redemptive act. But it's Siegfried, through Brünnhilde's forgiveness and sacrifice, who is cleansed of the curse he bore in behalf of Wotan. Siegfried embodied the fullness of the curse that came upon all because of Wotan's transgression. Brünnhilde's immolation is then broader than a simple redemptive act for the sake of a person, but for all. She brings to both mortal and immortal something beyond mere cleansing from the effects of the curse. When we broach this dimension, we move beyond mere forgiveness and cleansing, to death and rebirth; *transformation. Der Ring Des Nibelungen,* which we will refer to as *The Ring* from this point forward, thus deals with redemption, the cessation of the

"PARSIFAL: THE WILL AND REDEMPTION"

curse, and their causes. But in its final statement, both dramatically and musically, it also communicates rebirth of a new world.

In *Holländer*, Senta brings salvation and redemption to the Dutchman; which is straightforward and personal. In Tannhäuser, Elisabeth through her life of intercessory prayer attains from God what the Pope declared impossible, forgiveness and redemption for Tannhäuser; also straightforward and personal.

In *Lohengrin*, redemption is more complicated; needless to say the stage is being set for *The Ring*. By restoring young Gottfried as the Duke of Brabant, Lohengrin realizes for everyone Elsa's innocence and returns hope to the people. However, the transformation of Gottfried from the swan in the lake means several things, one of the most important is that it is a rebirth. Wagner broadens the message from simple redemption through an act of one person towards another, to redemption through rebirth and enlightenment.

In *Lohengrin* from the beginning of the opera to the end, the struggle for this rebirth lies between two forces; the pagan gods of Valhalla and the monotheistic God of the Grail. This conflict is personified through Ortrud and Lohengrin. While there is no real physical struggle, Ortrud has waged spiritual war against Lohengrin and all he represents because the people have left their worship of pagan gods and embraced what is presented as Christianity. In the second act, Ortrud attempts to deceive Elsa in doing the deed that would rid the land of Lohengrin and his *spiritual influence* by revealing his name, which to this point is kept secret. As one reads the libretto, take note of all Elsa's references to her Christian God, in contrast to Ortrud's gods.

ELSA
Before God, why do you reproach me? Was it I who brought this grief upon you?

ORTRUD
How indeed could you envy my fortune that the man you so lightly rejected should choose me for his wife?

ELSA
Gracious heaven! Why this to me?

ORTRUD
Misled by some fatal delusion, he was led to bring a charge against your innocence; now his heart is rent with remorse, and he is condemned to fearful punishment.

ELSA
O righteous God!

ORTRUD
Ah, you are happy! After brief undeserved suffering you see life only smiling on you; you can calmly turn away from me and consign me to the road to death, so that the sad sound of my distress shall never cloud your rejoicing!

ELSA
How little would I prize Thy blessings, Almighty God, who hast been so gracious to me, if I thrust from me the adversity which kneels before me in the dust! O never! Ortrud! Wait there for me! I myself will let you in! *(She hurries back into the Kemenate.)*

ORTRUD
(Springing up from the steps in fierce exaltation.) Now aid my vengeance, ye dishonored gods! Punish the disgrace brought upon you here! Strengthen me in the Service of your holy cause! Destroy the vile beliefs of the apostates! Wotan the mighty, I call on thee! Freia the sublime, hear me! Bless me with guile and deceit, that my revenge may be sweet!

(Lohengrin: Act II, Scene 2)

Lohengrin, unlike the earlier two operas, broadens redemption from simply one or two individuals to a spiritual dichotomy. By the conclusion of Act III, the fact that Gottfried *is the swan* that draws the boat which brought Lohengrin and is now returning him to the Grail's castle, makes for an interesting discussion. First, it was Ortrud who cast the spell on Gottfried and transformed him into the swan that propelled the boat. The correlation between what actually propelled Lohengrin and calls him into action are all intertwined. In the end, Ortrud makes her purposes clear:

> ORTRUD
> Go home! Go home, proud hero, and let me joyfully tell your foolish bride who it is that draws your boat! From the chains I wound around him I knew full well who this swan was: he is the heir of Brabant!
>
> ALL
> What!
>
> ORTRUD
> *(to Elsa)* My thanks for driving the knight away! The swan is carrying him homeward: had the hero stayed longer he would also have freed your brother!
>
> ALL
> Monster of womankind! What a crime you have admitted in your shameless exultation!
>
> ORTRUD
> See how the gods take their revenge for your having turned away from them!
>
> *(Lohengrin: Act III, Scene 3)*

Note Ortrud's statement, *"See how the gods take their revenge for your having turned away from them!"* Based on what is about to happen, this pending redemption is now changed from a simple redemption of a person (as in *Holländer* and *Tannhäuser*) to a spiritual conflict resulting in a metamorphosis. It's no longer about a redemption of a person, but a redemption and transformation of a people and their world. It's the initiation of a complete spiritual and cultural revolution from polytheism to monotheism.

The stage direction is equally telling, showing us that Ortrud *"... remains standing erect in savage ecstasy"*, while Lohengrin *"... now solemnly sinks to his knees in silent prayer ... The white dove of the Grail descends and hovers over the boat. Lohengrin perceiving it, springs up with a look of gratitude and unfastens the chain from the swan, whereupon it immediately plunges beneath the water. In its place Lohengrin lifts a handsome youth in gleaming silver garments - Gottfried - from the river on to the bank."*

First is the contrast of Ortrud's *savage ecstasy* and Lohengrin's *silent prayer*. While one is loud and fierce, it pales to the meditative, *peaceful* strength to Whom Lohengrin prays. The second is the expression of the swan plunging beneath the water and Gottfried arising in its place. This metamorphosis is displayed in the similitude of Christian baptism. It represents one's outer identification with their inner transformation. It's an external figure of inner death and rebirth.

Regarding the connections of Wagner's operas, the most obvious is the link when Lohengrin gives his horn, sword and ring to Elsa. These are undoubtedly the significant symbols of the coming hero Siegfried in *The Ring*. Not to mention the correlation of their names, Gottfried - Peaceful God, and Siegfried - Peaceful Victory. Regarding the symbolism of the swan, we will discuss this in detail as we progress to the appearance of Parsifal.

In one respect we can say that the last scene in *Lohengrin*, with the struggle between Ortrud's and Lohengrin's spiritual forces is expounded through the five operas of *The Ring* and *Parsifal*. As stated earlier, Valhalla comes crashing down in flames with gods and heroes in it, only to reemerge as Monsalvat with the knights of the Grail.

"PARSIFAL: THE WILL AND REDEMPTION"

In the closing scene of *Götterdämmerung* it becomes clear that Wotan is eternally guilty of his misconduct and destined for destruction. Yet when it comes to redemption, a messianic symbology occurs between Siegfried and Brünnhilde. Siegfried is that messianic archetype who embodies the guilt of another, similarly to Christ bearing the sins of humanity on the Cross. More specifically, Christ on the Cross bore the sin of Adam, who in turn brought the curse of sin and death to all. In the same way Siegfried bore the transgression of Wotan, which in turn also affected all.

Brünnhilde, the other half of the messianic equation, brings cleansing to her beloved and finality to the era of the pagan gods:

BRÜNNHILDE
O you, heavenly guardian of oaths! Turn your gaze on my great grief, see your everlasting guilt! Hear my lament, mighty god! Through his most formidable deed that you rightly desired, you sacrificed him who wrought it to the curse which had fallen on you: this innocent had to betray me so that I should become a woman of wisdom!
(Götterdämmerung: Act III, Scene 3)

Together, Brünnhilde and Siegfried bring redemption and forge a new age. The messianic concept of the union between the Divine Masculine and Feminine are found throughout much of eastern and western spirituality; like Shiva and Shakti in the East, and Christ and the Church (His Bride) in the West. In Siegmund's statement of how he came into the world, he said, *"I come into the world one of two ..."* **for rebirth to take place into a new reality requires the two to find each other and be united.** This concept will be important in *Parsifal*.

It could be said from a broader view that *The Ring* is really about redemption from pagan ignorance to Divine enlightenment. Brünnhilde in her immolation, states that through Siegfried's betrayal she has become a woman of wisdom. In the same manner Wotan in the third act of Siegfried gives us crucial insight to the connection:

> WOTAN
>
> To you, unwise one, I address these words so that you then may sleep carefree forever. Fear of the gods' downfall does not grieve me, since now I will it! What once I resolved in hopelessness, in the wild pain of dispute, now I will freely perform, gladly and joyously.
>
> Though in fury and abhorrence I flung the world to the Nibelung's envy, now to the valiant Wälsung I leave my inheritance. He whom I chose, though he does not know me, the bravest of youths, whom I have never advised, has gained the Nibelung's ring.
>
> Rejoicing in love, innocent of envy, his nobility will paralyze Alberich's curse for fear remains foreign to him. Brünnhilde, whom you bore me, will awaken to the hero: on waking, the child of your wisdom will do the deed that will redeem the world.
>
> So now sleep on, close your eyes: in dream behold my downfall! Whatever now befalls, to the ever-young the god in bliss yields. Descend then, Erda, mother of fear, of timeless sorrow! Away, away to endless sleep!
>
> *(Siegfried: Act III, Scene 1)*

Wotan says much here, yet to center on our point, he makes it clear he vehemently resisted the closing age of the gods, but now has accepted it with resolve. He is willing to relinquish his world to a new world, in Siegfried and Brünnhilde. He makes a point to say that Siegfried *rejoices in love and is innocent of envy,* something that the gods, dwarfs, giants and mankind under Wotan's rule were not. He adds that Brünnhilde will *awaken to the hero* and *on waking ... she will do the deed that will redeem the world.* To what, and when does Brünnhilde awaken? Her awakening begins at the conclusion of *Siegfried* Act III; however, it is not completed

"PARSIFAL: THE WILL AND REDEMPTION"

until the conclusion of *Götterdämmerung*. Here Siegfried is murdered, and in his final words prior to his physical death, he is conveyed to a higher spiritual world and completes Brünnhilde's waking:

> SIEGFRIED
> Brünnhilde! Holy bride! Awake! Open your eyes! Who sank you again in sleep? Who shackled you in uneasy slumber? Your wakener came and kissed you awake, and again broke the bride's bondage: Brünnhilde laughed in delight at him! Ah, her eyes, forever open! Ah, the blissful stirring of her breath! Sweet passing, blessed terror: Brünnhilde bids me welcome!
>
> *(Götterdämmerung: Act III, Scene 2)*

Through her awakening, Brünnhilde is now 'wise', and able to perform the redemptive act bringing a conclusion to the cursed world of the gods. The enlightenment now *known* by her is what brings the necessary ingredients for redemption and its path to transformation. Here again we find a *Parsifal* connection. The name 'Kundry' can be translated as, 'Known'. The name Gundryggia, is a Wagnerian manipulation of the Valkyrie's name and the cryptic translation of 'Known'. Thus, we have Gundry(ggia), the transformed Valkyrie, a pagan warrior maiden, now in a state of *knowing* ... Kundry. Eventually, as Kundry, she will be in a full state of enlightenment as she completes her journey. However, to bring her masculine counterpart, formerly Siegfried, now Parsifal, to his complete transformation and redemption, she provides the necessary catalyst for him to attain wisdom and become 'knowing' as well.

The same can be said of Wagner's operas *Tannhäuser* and *Die Meistersinger von Nürnberg* regarding reincarnations that merge into a *Parsifal*-like ending (see extended endnote[8]).

With the powerful connections mentioned regarding *Lohengrin* and *The Ring*, there are two very important characters in *Parsifal* that we have not yet mentioned; Amfortas and Klingsor.

Klingsor is the least obvious in connection to any of Wagner's prior operas, much less their villains. We may make some correlation to Alberich. He renounced love for the sake of gaining the ability to forge and access the power of the Ring. He also took that which was of 'nature', the gold, and *manipulated* it into a ring. You could correlate this first action with Klingsor mutilating (castrating) himself for the sake of sexual purity to gain the Grail. Of course this self-mutilation was rejected by the guardian of the Grail, Titurel, which only inflamed Klingsor's lust to possess it all the more. In addition, Klingsor does through the command of occultic power transform the natural world into that which is unnatural. Besides Alberich, there is his son Hagan in *Götterdämmerung*. The correlation here is that he does mortally wound our hero Siegfried with his spear, as did Klingsor to Amfortas. Klingsor is an amalgamation of all these personas. However, Klingsor hasn't attained godhood like Wotan, nor does he believe in any god. Rather, he utilizes the occult, which can be attributed to paganism, but he has no faith in the occult world from the perspective of those forces being deities. For him the occult, or magic is what he masters. As we will see in our discussion of *Parsifal*, Klingsor is an amalgamation of *The Ring* characters, plus an embodiment of latter-era Age of Enlightenment philosophy; in particular, the philosophy that Frederick Nietzsche and his contemporaries embraced. Thus, Klingsor is very much an unbeliever who has mastered the forces of nature for his own *Self-Willed* purposes.

With this in mind, we must take a moment to mention Wotan's correlation to Titurel, who is the godlike character of the work. He first possessed the Spear, long before the curtain rose. You could say he possessed it when, or as Wotan did. But more importantly, like Wotan he is, in a sense, a demigod. He built the sanctuary of the Grail for basically the same reasons that Wotan built Valhalla. Also Titurel and the knights live pseudo-eternally beholding the Grail, much like Wotan and the gods lived pseudo-eternally on Freia's golden apples.

Finally, we have Amfortas. Amfortas first came to Wagner's thoughts as far back as the mid 1850's (during the initial assembly of *The Ring*, and of *Tristan und Isolde)*. In one respect we see shadows of Amfortas in the deteriorating Wotan. But the strongest connection is to Tristan. Wagner himself said on May 30th, 1859:

> "... *It's Amfortas who is the center of attention ... It suddenly became awfully clear to me: it is my third-act of Tristan inconceivably intensified. With the spear-wound and perhaps another wound too, in his heart. The wretched man knows of no other longing in his terrible pain than the longing to die ...* "**9**

Wieland Wagner reported that his grandfather actually toyed with the idea of introducing the character of Parsifal to the ailing Tristan in Act III of *Tristan und Isolde.* Fortunately for all of us, Wagner abandoned the idea. Can you imagine Tristan with a different ending? Can you imagine no Isolde's Liebestod!? I don't want to even entertain the thought! Sing Isolde, sing!

To conclude, there is one other connection that must be mentioned here, which we will also refer to later, because this association helped shape the *Parsifal* we know. This is the clash between Wagner and his former long-time friend, Fredrick Nietzsche, by the time *Parsifal* was being performed at Bayreuth.

To begin with, it's important to point out that all of Nietzsche's published criticisms of Wagner, directly or indirectly, would occur *after* Wagner's death in 1883[10], though Wagner and Nietzsche parted ways in 1876.

One of the key issues of their parting was the spiritual and philosophical content within *Parsifal*. While Nietzsche was forming his forthcoming thesis of the ultimate übermensch, Zarathustra; Wagner was forming his. In the beginning Nietzsche and Wagner had similar thoughts regarding their two heroes, Zarathustra and Siegfried. But that would be short lived as Wagner found himself, to a measure, returning to his Christian roots. Siegfried reincarnated as Parsifal was a total horror for Nietzsche. The idea that Wagner, the genius and philosophical idol of Nietzsche, would embrace such 'weakness' as Christianity was too much to take. In the same year, Nietzsche would pen the following:

"It was indeed high time to say farewell: soon after, I received the proof. Richard Wagner, apparently most triumphant, but in truth a decaying and despairing decadent, suddenly sank down, helpless and broken, before the Christian cross. Did no German have eyes in his head or pity in his conscience for this horrid spectacle? Was I the only one whom it pained? Enough; this unexpected event struck me like lightening and gave me clarity about the place I had left - and also that shudder which everybody feels after he has unconsciously passed through a tremendous danger. As I proceeded alone I trembled; not long after, I was sick, more than sick, namely weary ... - weary from nausea at the whole idealistic lie and pampering of the conscience, which had here triumphed once again over one of the bravest ... I was henceforth sentenced ... to be more profoundly alone than ever before. For I had had nobody except Richard Wagner."[11]

To evoke such a reaction from Nietzsche, clearly Wagner's convictions must have been quite irrevocably clear. Yet, many today in their writings and productions of Wagner's *Parsifal* take *the Nietzsche approach*. We find Nietzsche's anti-

"PARSIFAL: THE WILL AND REDEMPTION"

Christian sentiment in a letter he wrote to his sister in early 1887:

> *"When listening to this music one lays Protestantism aside as a misunderstanding - and also, I will not deny it, other really good music, which I have at other times heard and loved, seems, as against this, a misunderstanding!"* [12]

While Wagner most definitely was not depicting what we will call for now, traditional Christianity, he also was not excluding and in fact appears to have been including what most would agree are elements of strong Christian influence in his music.

The Nietzsche approach is that Wagner's philosophy and his religious connotations are to be viewed as a *misunderstanding*, even though other music pales when held up to *Parsifal*. Thus, *Parsifal* was for Nietzsche some of the greatest music he'd ever heard. He augments this in an earlier letter saying, *"I wish I would have composed it myself"*. Yet in sharp contrast, he holds that one must also lay aside the Protestantism or Christian suggestions in Wagner's music as a misunderstanding. Hence *the Nietzsche approach* is to see the spiritual, and in particular the Christian implications as a misunderstanding, but the music as wonderfully grand. Sadly for many in the world of music this approach is now the status-quo, and in many productions is presented as such. However, when we make such myopic observations, and worse present them as fact, we no longer have *Wagner's Parsifal*.

It is no wonder why Wagner forbad his work to be performed in other opera houses for so many years! *To alter the text or the key aspects of the staging, was to alter the work and Wagner's intended message!*

So here we are, the foundation is laid; Valhalla is transfigured into Monsalvat, the Ring reformed into the Grail, Siegfried and Brünnhilde reincarnated as Parsifal and Kundry, the spiritual conflict of Ortrud and Lohengrin, recast between the occult and the Divine, Amfortas an augmented transformation of Tristan, and the Spear handed over from Wotan to Titurel and Klingsor.

We now settle in our seats, the lights dim in our inner theater, and the audience holds its breath in silent-expectancy...

"PARSIFAL: THE WILL AND REDEMPTION"

Vorspiel: Gesamtkunstwerk - Art Replaces Religion

Similar to *Das Rheingold's* quiet single E^b pedal note which opens the epic *Ring*, *Parsifal* also begins with a single note - A^b - which quietly emerges from the silence of the dark theater, and slowly ascends to C and then E^b forming the first three notes of the arpeggio of the tonic key of the opera. These three notes are also the beginning of the Communion leitmotif which then materializes before us. We are being transported from the carnal world of flesh and bone, to the eternal, otherworldly terrain of inner consciousness - the spirit. The direction in the orchestral score says, "Sehr Langsam, Sehr Ausdrucksvoll" which means, "Very Slowly, Very Expressive". This direction has more to it than simply defining a slower tempo than usual for an opera. For those familiar with meditation, if the cadence of the Prelude is taken at or below a metronome signature of 50, it mimics meditative breathing. In both the James Levine and Hans Knappertsbusch Bayreuth recordings of *Parsifal*, the Prelude hovers around this tempo; placing the Prelude length at approximately fourteen to sixteen minutes. The point is, we as members of the audience, tend to breathe within the cadence of the music we experience. Unknowingly to us, we are being invited by Wagner into a time of inner meditation.

Another interesting aspect of the *Parsifal* Prelude is that it doesn't start on the downbeat at the beginning of the measure. Instead, it begins on the upbeat. The Prelude is written in basic *4/4* time. In other words, each measure is counted in the basic form of *1 - 2 - 3 - 4*. The downbeat being - 1 - and the upbeats being - *2* - and - *4* -. Some composers start their compositions with a grace note or the last beat in the opening measure (which would be - *4* -) to accentuate the downbeat of the following measure beginning their musical statement. But here, Wagner uses neither a grace note, nor the last beat of a measure to accentuate the downbeat. Rather he simply starts on - *2* -. Why? In breathing, the downbeat is the exhale while the upbeat is the inhale. Wagner begins *Parsifal* with the suggestion to the audience to inhale followed by an exhale, much like how we focus our breathing as we enter contemplative meditation.

A final point about beginning the Prelude on the upbeat is that it appears to come out of nowhere. Rather than entering on the downbeat, like the emphatic statement of the Prelude to *Meistersinger*, this Prelude just appears; it simply materializes as if from another world. More so, it's not that it appears from another dimension, rather it's the audience that's transmigrating from one world to another.

This metaphysical world is shortly to take form on the stage before us. As of the single note that begins the Prelude, Wagner will bring the full power and authority of his honed craftsmanship of staging, poetry and music to bear on his audience and transport each initiate into the inner, infinite spiritual world we all occupy.

This artistry that Wagner employs is one of his own making, he called it, *Gesamtkunstwerk*, literally translated the *Total Art Work*. This concept is attached to Richard Wagner since he first penned the phrase in *The Art Work of the Future* and again later in *Art and Revolution*. Throughout his artistic life, both in opera and literature, this is what he conceptualized. Gesamtkunstwerk is not just the compilation, but the *synergism* of music, drama, poetry, dance and staging, including painting and set design. Thus, the Total Art Work creates a complete *synthesis of the senses.* Many modern productions do the opposite, intentionally deconstructing the unity of impact on the senses. Because of this, many Wagnerians who have tasted Gesamtkunstwerk are frustrated with the fragmented approach.

By the time we reach *Parsifal*, Wagner uses his synthesis of the senses to awaken what couldn't be sensed by any one of them. In other words, he awakens what couldn't be sensed through natural means. He awakens our inner sense of awareness, our sense of otherworldliness.

Wagner experienced the realization of Gesamtkunstwerk while forging *The Ring* in 1875 for the debut of the Bayreuth Festival. During that time, he returned to ponder his *Parsifal* once again and commenced his second draft in 1877; twenty years after it was first conceived. It's here the revelation of the Gesamtkunstwerk fusion is divulged. Wagner has found its ultimate purpose:

> *"... Art grasps the Figurative of an idea, that outer form in which it shows itself to the imagination, and by developing the likeness - before employed but by allegorically - into a picture embracing in itself the whole idea, she lifts the latter high above itself into the realm of revelation."*[13]

Wagner uses the synergy of Gesamtkunstwerk to awaken what could be termed a sixth sense, revealing *"the One Divinely True"*, the Spirit that has been buried by Religion. It is this 'hidden truth' which Art in general and music in particular, especially Wagner's music, has the capability to unveil. When we follow Wagner's thoughts, we must understand he was not saying that all Art reveals the Divine. Rather, Art has the potential to do so where Religion may have failed. For Art to reveal the Divine, if that is possible, it must be free from that which is common. Any distraction can detract from these aims, such as a retained reference to dogmatic symbols of religion, or even sharing the same stage with *the previous and following night's theatrical entertainment.* Therefore his *Parsifal*, which is intended to reveal that true Spirit free from the bondage of Religion or other impediments, was at first confined to Bayreuth. He made this apparent on September 28, 1880:

> *"I should certainly not blame our Church authorities if they were to raise an entirely legitimate protest against representations of the most sacred mysteries upon the selfsame boards on which yesterday and tomorrow, frivolity sprawls in luxuriant ease before an audience attracted solely by such frivolity. I was entirely right in feeling that I should entitle 'Parsifal' a 'Sacred Stage Festival'. And must now try to consecrate a stage for it, and can only be my solitary festival theater in Bayreuth. There and there alone may 'Parsifal' be presented now and always: never shall Parsifal be offered in any other theater as an amusement for its audience: and to ensure that this happens I am uniquely concerned at present and persuaded to consider how and by what I may safeguard the destiny of this work."*[14]

There we have it! Gesamtkunstwerk is not simply the combination of music, drama, poetry, dance and set design, it also unveils the *Divine Spirit*. Surely other composers have works with those ingredients; even Wagner has those elements in his first three operas: *Die Feen, Das Liebesverbot,* and *Rienzi*.

You could say that to Wagner, this kind of Gesamtkunstwerk can be accomplished only with perfect chemistry. Like anything we bake, the cake will not rise if the ingredients are disproportioned. If the ultimate purpose of Art through Gesamtkunstwerk is to save the Spirit which is trapped by Religion; then according to Wagner, two things were necessary. First, there must be perfect chemistry, and second, an initiated audience. The fact that he confined *Parsifal* to Bayreuth was to protect just that, *the chemistry and the audience.*

The aim is clear. Confining *Parsifal* to its intended chemistry and initiation only within the Bayreuth Festival Theater, and separating it from and keeping it away from other entertainment at regular opera houses, would preserve its envisioned purpose.

With that in mind, how do you *initiate* someone who doesn't know they need initiating? Not to mention, seeing something that is intended to be divined, and is not meant only for amusement? The answer is: *create the desire.* Please note that Wagner's approach is not arbitrary; it is well thought out. According to esoteric teachings, especially Christianity and Buddhism, the only way to receive Divine truth is to create the necessary desire for it through resistance and difficulty. Wagner employed that concept to create such desire. We will discuss more on this when we speak of Parsifal's journey.

Unlike any other of Wagner's works which could be seen at any opera house willing to put on a production, he made *Parsifal* arduous to experience. This work couldn't be seen anywhere - only in Bayreuth. To see *Parsifal* it took real effort. He *created the desire* for his audience to experience it by making it exclusive. In so doing, he imparted value and importance to it, and transformed going to *Parsifal* into a *pilgrimage.* Even if you'd seen *The Ring* elsewhere, or heard excerpts of it at a concert in Europe, you still had to go to Bayreuth to experience *Parsifal*, an opera you perhaps had only heard about through rumor. Remember that we are speaking of well over 100 years ago; travel was not easy or comfortable. By doing all this, Wagner transformed the Festival into a quasi-religious experience. After all the travel, you finally walked or rode your horse and buggy up the only road that led to the Green Hill. Think of the context of Tannhäuser's long grueling journey to Rome and then back to his homeland seeking absolution.

    There, high upon the hill towered the theater overlooking the city. It was like going to church or temple. Yet unlike a church or temple where you might be greeted with worshipful music, as you traveled up this hill, there was a deafening silence and anticipation, which made it all the more exhilarating. It created an expectancy that was not felt in one's daily life. Finally, as you neared the theater, the silence gave way to a low humming sound of other pilgrims like yourself in eager conversation. They were waiting for members of the orchestra brass section to mount the theatre balcony and begin playing the opening notes of the Communion motif to summon you to your seat. There is no lobby with lavish hallways leading you to fancy plush seats. Rather, just like a temple or church, you would enter a short foyer, climb some stairs, and enter the hallowed chamber. By being in the theater-made-sanctuary, the low murmurs you heard outside increased in volume as you stood waiting for everyone in your row to be seated. There are no aisles to walk through to get to your seat. Just long, arching rows from the side door you entered, to the entry door on the other end of the long row. Finally, once everyone in your row has taken their place, you could sit. You were now with other pilgrims just like yourself in a unified and rarified anticipation. Then the lights dim exactly on time, and darkness fills the consecrated hall; your body can feel the anticipation flowing through every limb. The rumble of voices hush, there is that deafening silence again - but not for long. As the prelude seemingly emerges out of the darkness, you have arrived. You feel the embrace of the experience as if you held the love of your life for the first time.

    The days of travel, the discomfort of the journey, virtually relocating your life for a short period; the title 'Sacred

Stage Festival' makes total sense. The unsuspecting pilgrim was finally ready for what was about to take place. By pressing through the difficulty and the building of all the expectation, fashioned a desire within to receive what was to be revealed. The unknowing initiate was prepared to see what could not be easily seen.

Wagner writes, when he was first contemplating *Parsifal*: "... *he who would know of it must hear in my works themselves what superficial listeners cannot hear.*" *(September 1865)*[15]

It's important to mention that at the second Bayreuth Festival in 1882, Parsifal was the only opera performed, following *The Ring* in 1876. Thus, Wagner's central five operas were first premiered at Bayreuth. Once again, the reality of what we discussed in the previous chapter echoes; the Nibelung drama built the environment for *Parsifal*. What one might consider a significant point of Bayreuth trivia is that at the time this author penned these pages in 2014, *Parsifal* will have been performed at the Festival 513 times, more than double that of *The Ring* or any other opera.

The Prelude engulfs us, and reality of another world overtakes us. The dichotomy of Ortrud and Lohengrin is unfolding. Something that was not mentioned previously has reason to be mentioned now - the definition of the names Ortrud and Lohengrin. Let's not forget that Lohengrin in the final scene of the opera that bears his name will bring forth Gottfried transformed from the swan and offer his ring, sword and horn - all pointing toward the coming Siegfried in *The Ring*. Equally as important, prior to bringing forth Gottfried, Lohengrin proclaims, *"I was sent to you by the Grail, my father Parsifal wears its crown"*. Lohengrin's father is the source of the transformation.

The name Lohengrin comes from the words *lohe* and *grinst*, blazing flame and smile (grin or smirk). When you put them together you have *grinning* or *smiling flame*. This is in reference to the *tongues of fire* and *the wind of the Spirit* in the New Testament, which appears at Pentecost, when the Holy Spirit arrives filling the 120 disciples in the Upper Room. This usually receives little reference when discussing *Parsifal*. However, similarly, prior to *Tristan und Isolde*, Wagner explored both poetically, musically and conceptually the drama's construction through the Wesendonck Lieder. In the case of *Parsifal*, Wagner wrote a symphonic choral piece in 1843 called, *Das Liebesmahl der Apostel (The Love-Feast of the Apostles)*. This would be one of the key sources he would explore in mood and structure for his final work. An interesting aspect of the work is that there is approximately 45 minutes of *a cappella* choral work as the apostles await the arrival of the Holy Spirit. When the Spirit arrives, the tongues of fire and rushing wind, the orchestra appears and erupts for the first time.

DISCIPLES
What rushing fills all the air! What sounds! What voices! And stirs not the very ground upon which we stand? Be greeted by us, Spirit of the Lord; your breath we feel around our heads and mightily you fill all our souls.

(Das Liebesmahl der Apostel)

While we have the *smiling flames* of the Holy Spirit on the one side, we have Ortrud on the other. Ortrud means, *serpentine,* or that which *resembles the serpent.* It's the age-old contrast of the Serpent and the Spirit. *The Ring* and *Parsifal*, on the other hand, is not just about the conflict of the two, as in *Lohengrin*, but the metamorphosis of the *one into the other.* The pagan, polytheistic world of the gods is yielding to an all-encompassing monotheistic God. It is the transformation of the conflicted Norse, Germanic gods and the besieged world they ruled into a new age led by the encompassing God of Compassion. For Wagner this is the central theme. This transformation is echoed by Wotan who said, *"Whatever now befalls, to the ever-young the god in*

"PARSIFAL: THE WILL AND REDEMPTION"

bliss yields." The ever-young, were Siegfried and Brünnhilde, captivated by love and it would be the wisdom gained by compassionate suffering (Brünnhilde's awakening) that would create the metamorphosis from one world to the next. Wagner was very clear on July 14, 1879 regarding his definition of compassion. This was not just good theater, but something he truly believed philosophically and spiritually:

> *"Man evidently begins to exist with the entry of deceit into the powerful series of the development of beings; God will have revealed Himself with the entry of the most unshakeable truth into every domain of existence: the way from man to Him is compassion and its eternal name is, Jesus."*[16]

Some commentators, taking the Nietzsche approach mentioned earlier, have said when discussing *Parsifal* that *Christ* is never mentioned in the text and therefore is not really related to the work. First, it's true the word 'Christ' is never mentioned in the text. Yet, neither is there mention of the sword *Nothung*, the symbol of Wotan's grand idea, in *Das Rheingold*. But, it's clearly announced in the music after Wotan sings:

WOTAN
It's approaching the night, from envy it now offers shelter.

(as taken from a great idea, very determined)

So I greet the castle safe from grief and horror.

(He turns solemn to Fricka)

(Das Rheingold: Scene 4)

It's during the stage directions where it says, *"as taken from a great idea ..."* and *"He turns solemn to Fricka"*. The leitmotif of the Sword, the symbol of Wotan's grand idea is announced. As we progress we will find that when Wagner discussed *Parsifal*, he appears to always have had Jesus Christ in mind. For example, he wrote to King Ludwig on August 11th 1873:

> "... I am inspired to write this work in order to preserve the world's profoundest secret, the truest Christian faith, nay, to awaken that faith anew."[17]

Wagner was not a proponent of the Christian religion in the traditional sense, any more than he was a proponent of the Buddhist religion, or any other for that matter. Rather, Wagner in a sense was able to penetrate their traditions and rituals and extract the essence of what they communicated. Over time, he focused more on Christianity because it encompassed and even surpassed other religions, as far as he was concerned. For him Christianity in the sense of its central theme even surpassed Schopenhauer:

> "In this respect we can but regard it as a sublime distinction of the Christian religion, that it expressly claims to bear the deepest truth to the 'poor in spirit', for their comfort and their salvation; whereas the doctrine of the Brahmins was the exclusive property of 'those who know' ... That there was a shorter road to salvation; the most enlightened of the 'Reborn' himself disclosed to the poor blind Folk: but the sublime of renunciation and unruffled meekness, which the Buddha set, did not suit his followers. ... It was otherwise with the Christian religion. Its founder was not wise, but divine, his teaching was indeed of free-willed suffering. To believe in him, meant to emulate him; to hope for redemption, to strive for union with him."[18]

This is why the Prelude to *Parsifal* begins with the leitmotif of Communion. The Communion in Christian spirituality identifies with the sacrificial suffering of Christ through compassion and allows entry into the spirit of his resurrected life. It brings transformational components to the inner life, compared to ritual just for ritual sake, or to the

"PARSIFAL: THE WILL AND REDEMPTION"

Brahmin (and Buddhist) doctrine where this special knowledge was the exclusive property only of 'those who know'. In the same breath, however, Wagner explores Buddhism as far as possible, employing his knowledge of the Norse and Teutonic myths, finding those complimentary to his understanding of what true Christianity is. He then merges them together. In so doing, the curtain rises and the realization of *Parsifal* Act I appears before our eyes. We began perhaps as members of an audience attending an opera, but now we are *observers of our inner selves* with all its spiritual qualities, contrasts and contradictions.

The curtain slowly rises ...

"EXPLORING RICHARD WAGNER'S FINAL TREATISE"

"PARSIFAL: THE WILL AND REDEMPTION"

ACT I

"PARSIFAL: THE WILL AND REDEMPTION"

Part I: The Domain of Religion

We see a lovely forest, two young squires apparently asleep while on duty, and our spiritual guide, Gurnemanz, in prayer. He awakens the young men:

GURNEMANZ
Ho there! You guardians of the woods, or rather of sleep, at least wake at morn!

Do you hear the call? Give thanks to God that you are called to hear it!

So to whom is this herald really proclaimed? To you and me, of course! We are being called to awaken our inner self, as we see our inner world portrayed on stage. We, who are supposed to be keenly aware of our spiritual perimeter, the forest that encompasses our deep inner sanctuary, are to now awake. But like the squires, many of us are not the guardians of that which is within us. Rather we sleep not paying attention to what really matters in the inner world. Our awareness is only of that which will appease us in the world of the senses, the world of matter.

One of the most deceptive vices that can be found among the multitude of the more obvious ones like the pride and arrogance which condemned the Dutchman to sail the seas; the sexual exploits of Tannhäuser which banned him from his fellow knights and Rome; the deceit and false accusations of Telramund; the forsaking of love for world domination by Alberich; or the building of an empire by sleight of hand and broken promises like Wotan. While these are terrible vices, they are sins in Christianity and deeds fit for bad karma in Buddhism. But to Wagner, the most deceptive of all these vices is *religion.* Why? - because of religion's intoxicating numbness, which causes a spiritual slumber within us.

The notion of religion in Wagner's context is not used in a positive regard, rather it is contrasted to spirituality. Religion, as we will explore, represents everything the Serpent offered the woman in the Garden in the Biblical account in *Genesis*. Thus, we are oblivious to our true deeper spiritual self, which we are told is wounded with a wound that cannot heal. Gurnemanz then tells the squires to tend to the bath for the ailing King Amfortas. From the very outset we know the answer and conclusion to the drama:

GURNEMANZ
We're fools to challenge hope for relief when only healing can bring relief. In vanity we search and hunt through the world for every medicine, there is only one that can help him - only one man.

No sooner does Gurnemanz mention the only man who can help the ailing King, Kundry arrives, riding wildly on her mare, shouting:

KUNDRY
Here! Take this! - Balsam ...

Soon there will be talk about the knight Gawain who went searching for an ointment that would bring, at the very most, minor relief to Amfortas. When Amfortas hears he ventured off, Amfortas is angry. Why? Amfortas is very familiar with venturing off when one is not commissioned by the Grail. He knows firsthand because of such zeal the results are folly and a wound that cannot be healed.

"PARSIFAL: THE WILL AND REDEMPTION"

But here we see Kundry, one who actually has attempted, and successfully might we add, to return and bring some form of balm of relief. Kundry is very consistent. Her words from the beginning of Act III say it all:

KUNDRY
Serve ... Serve!

Kundry is the most aware of the unseen underlying truths. While Amfortas is in torment in the obvious sense and knows why he's been wounded, Kundry is aware of the forces and inner workings as to why things have happened. While she is the most aware, she is also the most tormented character in the unfolding drama. Her *knowing* causes her torment. She also has a wound that will not heal, or better said, *she is the wound that will not heal.* While we don't actually see her wound, as we do with that of Amfortas, she is the most defined about what inner torment is.

Regarding Kundry, the opening dialogue with Gurnemanz and the squires in a broad sense is a depiction of religion in the most unspiritual use of the word. Kundry knows of her transgressions, although we as observers haven't yet learned what they all are. For her *at this point,* there are three key things that express her condition:

First, her wild pursuit to right her wrongs.

Second, her complete sense of unworthiness.

Third, her sense of doing good deeds to attain inner peace and union with God, which only creates more inner turmoil.

The last point above is the key to Wagner's view of religion in general - that it is an exasperating inner turmoil born of an obsessive desire to right our wrongs, in hopes of alleviating a deep sense of unworthiness and separation. This is at the core of our spiritual slumber, which erects the edifice of an artificial religious life concealing the One Divinely True.[19] The result is a *Will* to embrace dogma, leading to a sense of self-righteousness, rather than genuine inner transformation. This we will find is the true condition of the Grail knights. Kundry thus seeks to appease her inner-wound by doing whatever works of service she can find. Her greatest hope is to receive relief by attaining the ultimate approval; bringing healing to Amfortas. In the artificial religious life, we desire our efforts to be recognized either by the clergy we serve, who are supposed to be God's representatives, or by some sign or expression from the Divine itself.

A problem however arises, in that our inner-wound never heals; we never seem to be good enough to be granted complete relief. Hence, we fail and return to the cycle, trying yet again to achieve it. On the other hand, recognition from God's representative creates a dangerous precedent: we will do almost anything for our religious leader or our religion, if asked. We serve that leader or religion not necessarily because we are filled with Divine love and want to share it with others, but because we are trying to attain from religiosity what only the Divine really can give. Therefore, we serve the representative in hope that we can receive the relief we seek in some manner or by some pronouncement.

Consequently, we will do whatever we must do to right our wrongs, find inner peace, and most importantly, find acceptance in the Divine. The problem with such religious 'vice', especially from Wagner's point of view, is that both the Buddhist and Christian religious systems press one to never-ending doing of good deeds to expiate the evil deeds, motivated by fear and guilt. In addition to this never-ending cycle, the grip of such vice tightens further by religious hierarchy over the common man. While Wagner loved Buddhism, Hinduism and Christianity in their purest sense, he had interesting things to say about all three:

> *"The Brahminic (and its off shoot Buddhism)[20] religion we surely must rank as the most astounding evidence of the breadth of view and faultless mental*

accuracy of those earlier Aryan branches ... It had only one fault: it was a race-religion."[21]

The Brahminic religion, what we would now call Hinduism, is from Wagner's point of view a *caste* system. He also earlier considered Buddhism to be a *caste* system because its followers, in his view lacked compassion and pity for the suffering of others. For that matter, despite whatever karmic cycles were to follow, one was in a particular situation and caste because of the system's lack of compassion and pity, not necessarily because negative karma. Any attempt to break out of the caste allotted to you would only result in further negative karma. Some may feel that they are compassionate by leaving others in their lower-caste state so their karma can be worked out. But not Wagner; for him, to have compassion on another is to have compassion on the greater ideal of self. This we will unravel as the opera continues.

In this opening act we see a caste system. Kundry is at its lowest level. For that matter, women in the entire opera are generally regarded negatively. They are temptresses, sorceresses, and she-devils. This is what the caste system projects. However, in the mind of Wagner, women like Senta, Elizabeth, and most importantly Brünnhilde, were nothing of the sort; they were the key to salvation.

Here we meet Kundry riding wildly to the point of exhaustion as she tries to bring healing to the afflicted Grail King, Amfortas. The squires, on the other hand, depict a more superficial aspect of religion. Though they are the lowest in their class in the pecking order of traditional religion, they were a rung higher overall than Kundry. The drama opens with them asleep, but no sooner than Kundry arrives they become full of so-called wisdom. Their sleeping on the proverbial job is an indication of their spiritual dullness. Because of it they are quick to judge Kundry by her external behavior and to ascribe intention to her motives:

4th SQUIRE
With your magic balm, I suspect, you would try to harm our master.

GURNEMANZ
... she never approaches you, nor has she anything in common with you; yet when help is wanted in danger, her zeal speeds her through the air, and she never calls you for thanks ...

3rd SQUIRE
But she hates us! See how sneeringly she looks at us!

4th SQUIRE
She's a pagan sorceress!

Herein we see Wagner's love-hate relationship with religion. There is just enough evidence to jump off the cliff of suspicion and accusation without knowing Divine reality. *"I suspect you would harm our master".* There was no evidence of this, and Kundry's motive was the complete opposite in that moment. *"See how sneeringly she looks at us!"* There is truth in that declaration, but not because she is a hater of people. Rather, like most that deal with the accusations of religion, Kundry simply detests their judgments and condemnations. *"She's a pagan sorceress!"* again a partial truth. While she may appear to be some kind of sorceress, she is actually under the intermittent control of a powerful sorcerer. We will soon find out in the second act what real spell she is under.

During that exchange we hear Gurnemanz explain how she zealously serves the knights of the Grail and yet asks nothing in return. While there are many in the world of religion who accuse and condemn, there are as many who serve asking nothing in return; well, nothing we can obviously see. But they do ask, and not for something all that simple. They, through their deeds and service ask to be freed from their inner torment, guilt, condemnation and unworthiness. This is a poisonous combination for a caste system. It puts one in the position of believing they are where they are because of their guilt or some other infirmity. Then if it is suggested that one must do some act of service, especially in behalf of those higher in the system, oppression results.

When it came to Christianity, Wagner was swift to make his point (segment taken from the earlier letter quoted on July 14, 1879):

> *"There is nothing I would say about the Church except that, if Christianity had already been a living part of it, the Church has utterly destroyed it."*[22]

In the context of this letter, what Wagner detested was what the Catholic and much of the Protestant Church had done to 'pure Christianity'. These issues would be rehearsed through several additional letters and writings. One major issue was with the description of God within the Christian Church as being revealed as the God of the Old Testament. Wagner couldn't reconcile within his thinking that the Law giving, angry, accusing God that condemned mankind to death for not keeping the Law he gave, is the same God who came as the Christ. Wagner contrasts Jesus Christ to the former, as the one who willfully gave Himself to suffer under the hand of such condemnation for humanities redemption.[23] Similarly, the other issue for Wagner was the caste system at the root of Hinduism and Buddhism. While, in theory, in the Christian religion there wasn't a race-based caste system, there was effectively a caste system based on a hierarchy which kept the common seeker of religious truth in a sort of religious bondage. Within the *Parsifal* drama, Wagner doesn't attempt to resolve his conflicts with the God of the Old Testament in contrast to the New. Rather he addresses the broader issues culminating in his depiction of 'pure Christianity'.

Kundry reveals that all her service and deeds of heroism, going to and fro seeking relief for the wound she caused, is pointless. In other words, doing good deeds, keeping rituals for the sake of inner transformation is futile.

Wagner is telling us traditional religion in itself is pointless, regardless of its origins. Attempting to work for our absolution and to attain some sense of inner peace actually is what causes the affliction. *It keeps the wound open.*

Amfortas is then given the vial that holds the temporary relief:

AMFORTAS
You Kundry? Have I to thank you again you restless, timorous maid? Well then! I will try your balsam now: let this be thanks for your devotion.

Wagner is making a definitive statement about our sense and need for penance, as well as our propensity to live by rules to attain some form of divinity. Wagner says in *Religion and Art*:

> "Among the poorest and most distant from the world appeared the Savior, no more to reach redemptions path by precept, but example; his flesh and blood he gave as last and highest expiation for all the sin of outpoured blood and slaughtered flesh, and offered his disciples wine and blood for each day's meal: - 'Taste such alone, in memory of me'. This the unique sacrament of the Christian faith; with its observance of all the teaching of the Redeemer is fulfilled. As if with haunting pangs of conscience the Christian Church pursues this teaching, without ever being able to get it followed in its purity, although it very seriously should form the most intelligible core of Christianity."[24]

Like the typical religious person seeking spirituality, Kundry is trying to absolve herself of her condition by "doing the right things", but needless to say they are useless. Kundry lies on the ground before Amfortas to prostrate herself in service and humility. Sadly, one of the so-called superior squires degrades Kundry:

3rd SQUIRE
Hey, you there! Why do you lie there like a wild beast?

KUNDRY
Are not the beasts not holy here?

At this juncture, spirituality, redemption and healing is obscure to us, the observer. Kundry is a wild woman, Amfortas seems to be the wounded hero, and the squires are asking religious questions. The squires are saying and doing what some of us might do. Yet they are oblivious to Kundry's suffering. Thus, because they do not see, they are still slumbering. In the pride of their religious status above the wild woman, they are incapable of Divine compassion. Then Gurnemanz asks the pivotal question:

GURNEMANZ
Hey! You! Listen and tell me: Where were you roaming when our master lost the Spear? Why didn't you help us then?

KUNDRY
I ... never help.

She constantly tries to absolve herself of her wound, which is to heal the wound of Amfortas; regardless of how hard she tries, she fails, *she never helps!* What torment!

Gurnemanz then explains the revelation of the Grail and its origins to the squires. Titurel, father of Amfortas, was entrusted with both holy relics, Spear and Grail. After Christ died on the Cross, the attending centurion, Longinus, used his *spear* to pierce Christ's side to assure His death; this is now the holy Spear. Joseph of Arimathea, a member of the Sanhedrin and secret disciple of Jesus, was present to take Christ's body for burial. When Christ's side was pierced, Joseph of Arimathea had a *cup* which we call the Grail; it was used to catch the blood that flowed. There is much to speak of the Grail at this point; Wagner was not ignorant of its origins beyond Christianity. He writes to Mathilde Wesendonck on May 30th, 1859:

> *"That this miraculous object should be a precious stone is a feature which, admittedly, can be traced back to the earliest sources, namely the Arabic text of the Spanish Moors. One notices, unfortunately, that all our Christian legends have a foreign, pagan origin. As they gazed on in it in amazement, the early Christian learned, namely, that the Moors in the Caaba at Mecca deriving from the pre-Muhammadan religion venerated a miraculous stone, sunstone - or meteoric stone - but at all events one that had fallen from heaven. However, the legends of its miraculous power were soon interpreted by the Christians after their own fashion ..."* [25]

Wagner makes a distinction in his writings between Christian legends and their spiritual truth. For Wagner, as we will soon see, religion in the ritualistic sense, as well as its symbols and legends mean little; except that to many in Christianity and beyond, they meant much. For Wagner, the legends and symbols only serve as a vehicle for the truth he desires to show. Nevertheless, his task is daunting. He will use the symbols and legends and at the same time attempt to strip them away to open what they're intended to reveal.

This is what the knights and the squires represented. They, like many of us, are 'merely' religious. We are either enamored by or dismissive of symbols and legends, leaving inner truths undiscovered. Like our squires, who are slumbering when they should be observant, our knights are in essence no different. However, their spiritual sense is even duller. They will go through the ritual of Holy Communion, receive the sacrament of the bread and wine, and be willing to go forth and fight for the cause of the Grail; yet all the while numb to the pain of Amfortas.

"PARSIFAL: THE WILL AND REDEMPTION"

Gurnemanz continues his story of the Grail origins. We're told of Titurel, who was entrusted with the true reality of the relics meaning.

GURNEMANZ
... the Savior's angelic messengers descended one holy, solemn night; bearing the sacred vessel, the holy, noble cup from which He drank at the last supper, into which His divine blood flowed on the Cross and with it the Spear that shed it - these wondrous holy relics they gave into our King's charge.

So, what do the Spear and Grail represent? One may argue that they are just symbols of Christian legend. True, but now Wagner's daunting task of using them and then refocusing the observer from their symbolism to their Divine truths is afoot.

To set the stage for *Parsifal*, Wagner used the symbols of the Grail legends and history. However, if we were to use those legends and historical provenance as sole reference, we run into trouble discerning Wagner's intentions and message. In the construct of *The Ring*, he undoubtedly used the famous *Die Nibelungen-Geschichte*.[26] Yet he didn't just retell old legends and stories, line-by-line; contrasting, for example, to what Lerner and Loewe did, who faithfully created *My Fair Lady* from George Bernard Shaw's *Pygmalion*. Similarly, in Grail legend there isn't a female to be found with the wild characterization of Kundry; the closest we have is in Wolfram von Eschenbach's poem where there is a female character, Kondrie, but the resemblance is in name only. As we pointed out previously, Kundry's etymology comes with a dual connection to the Valkyrie, Gundry(ggia) and its cryptic translation of 'Known'. Yet, for Wagner, Kundry is a central figure.

Wagner also wasn't thrilled about Christian legends having pagan origins. Quoting from the letter mentioned earlier, Wagner said, *"One notices, unfortunately, that all our*

Christian legends have a foreign, pagan origin". Note that Wagner makes a distinction between paganized Christian legend and Christ of the New Testament.

Hence, Wagner used existing legends and symbols that were well suited to connect with his audience, but he did not rely upon them. His ultimate plan was to communicate his own intentions, and to that end he freely departed from his source materials, and of course, worked his magic of Gesamtkunstwerk.

In similar manner, as the slumbering squires misperceive Kundry, Wagner has been misapplied to secret societies and occult religions. Wagner has been implicated with Rosicrucianism, the Masons, the Templars, the Thule Society, and many more. Wagner is also mentioned in the bestselling conspiracy-theory book, *Holy Blood, Holy Grail*. It tells us that the Grail legends inspired Wagner to visit Rennes-le-Chateau, where the secrets of the Grail are kept.[27] Supposedly, according to local legend, Wagner also had an illegitimate child there. Whether or not Wagner visited Rennes-le-Chateau, or was a member of the myriad of secret societies that claim his affiliation, Wagner's Sacred Stage Drama was written with the legends and symbols in place, only to remove their veil and speak the spiritual truths he desired to communicate.

What is interesting about the actual artifacts, if they were to be found, is that they never really left the physical world. The cup that Christ used was just an ordinary cup used on the Sabbath. The supposed spear of Longinus, which was used to pierce the side of Christ, is in the Imperial Treasury at Hofburg Palace in Vienna, Austria. (A photograph of the spear is on the back of this book.) It even has a nail attached to it with an inscription that says the *"Nail of our Lord."*[28] The point being, the spear is still earthbound - has never left the physical world, and Wagner knew this. But what of the legend and the metaphors? What is the legend trying to communicate by saying that they descended from the heavens, and what then is Wagner trying to communicate by them?

Focusing on both legend and the Biblical account, we can see hints of his intentions. Wagner, gives a description of what his *Parsifal* Prelude means as it beckons to the audience:

> "Prelude of Parsifal: Love - Faith - Hope? First theme: Love. 'Take ye my body, take my blood, in token of our love!' (Repeated in faint whispers by angel-voices.) 'Take ye my blood, my body take, in memory of me!' (Again repeated in whispers.)"

> "Second theme: Faith. Promise of redemption through faith. Firmly and stoutly faith declares itself, exalted, willing even in suffering. - To the promise renewed Faith answers from the dimmest heights - as on the pinions of this snow-white dove - hovering downwards - usurping more and more the hearts of men, filling the world, the world of Nature with the mightiest force, then glancing up again to the heavens vault as the appeased. But once more, from out the awe of solitude, throbs forth the cry of loving pity: the agony, the holy sweat of Olivet, the divine death-throes of Golgotha - the body pales, the blood flows forth, and glows now in the chalice with the heavenly glow of blessing, shedding on all that lives in languishes the grace of ransom won by Love ..."[29]

Here, in this very early description of the Prelude, Wagner reiterates the events of Christ's death on the Cross. Some have objected in the interpretation of Parsifal having a 'Christian' focus, saying that the word *Christ* is never mentioned, and therefore is not the focus of the work. However, in Wagner's writings Parsifal and Christ are irrevocably joined. Another Biblical reference upon which the Grail legends and Parsifal are linked, is in the account of the Centurion Longinus piercing Christ's side:

"Then the soldiers came and broke the legs of the first and of the other who was crucified with Him. But when they came to Jesus and saw that He was already dead, they did not break His legs. But one of the soldiers pierced His side with a spear, and immediately blood and water came out. And he who has seen has testified, and his testimony is true; and he knows that he is telling the truth, so that you may believe."[30]

The focal point here is, *"... one of the soldiers pierced His side with a spear, and immediately blood and water came out"*. The legends state that the historical and biblical figure of Joseph of Arimathea, took the Cup and caught the flowing blood of the Savior; Gurnemanz also makes a direct reference to this in Act I.

Once again in the New Testament we find an important figure in Christ compared to Adam that Wagner will reference later:

"And so it is written, 'The first man Adam became a living being.' The last Adam became a life-giving spirit."[31]

Jesus Christ is called by the Apostle Paul, *"The last Adam ..."*. This designation is significant in many respects to the total of scripture. In our focus, what would be the significance of the Last Adam having His side pierced and opened? To understand that we have to refer to the first Adam:

"And the Lord God caused a deep sleep to fall on Adam, and he slept; and He took one of his ribs, and closed up the flesh in its place. Then the rib which the Lord God had taken from man He made into a woman, and He brought her to the man."[32]

Eve came out of the side of the first Adam, his bride and counterpart. From the side of the Last Adam came his bride and counterpart, the Ecclesia - in the purest sense of the meaning, those of humanity who receive and walk in His likeness, His Church. In Act II, Wagner makes a direct correlation to Adam and Christ in this respect when it comes to Kundry's kiss. We will look at that in detail later.

The revelation of the Divine is then encapsulated in the book of *Genesis* with the following verse:

> *"So God created Man in His own image; in the image of God He created him; male and female He created them."*[33]

As we stated in the previous chapter both in Eastern and Western spirituality the Divine is depicted in the unity of masculine and feminine spiritual qualities. In addition, when you think of Christianity, as well as the Old Testament, we must remember that the origin of its spirituality is Eastern. It wasn't until the time of Constantine and the assimilation of the Church into the Roman Empire that Christianity was really westernized. This is why Wagner writes about the Church in the manner he does. This is also why he finds a great congruency with Buddhism and Christianity in their purist sense.

The Bride of Christ that came from His side is archetyped for a brief moment in the same New Testament Gospel by the Apostle John through Mary Magdalene:

> *"But Mary stood outside by the tomb weeping, and as she wept she stooped down and looked into the tomb. ... she turned around and saw Jesus standing there, and did not know that it was Jesus. Jesus said to her, 'Woman, why are you weeping? Whom are you seeking?' She, supposing Him to be the gardener, said to Him, 'Sir, if You have carried Him away, tell me where You have laid Him, and I will take Him away'. Jesus said to her, 'Mary!' She turned and said to Him, 'Rabboni!' (which is to say, Teacher). Jesus said to her, 'Do not cling to Me, for I have not yet ascended to My*

Father; but go to My brethren and say to them, "I am ascending to My Father and your Father, and to My God and your God." Mary Magdalene came and told the disciples that she had seen the Lord, and that He had spoken these things to her."[34]

Like the first Adam who was in a garden from whose side came forth his feminine counterpart, now Christ, the Last Adam, is in a garden. When Mary first speaks with Him, she doesn't recognize who He is. She only 'sees' a gardener. Christ then calls her by name, Mary. In that moment her eyes are opened and she recognizes Jesus. He then commissions her to tell his disciples that she has seen Him and has risen.

There is an important point here to be made for later: when the first call of wakening comes to Parsifal, it is in the second act when Kundry *calls him by name* in the garden. This is obviously the reverse of what happened when Jesus calls Mary by name. In the Gospel the Masculine calls the Feminine, and in the second act of *Parsifal*, the Feminine calls the Masculine. The reason for this is that Wagner is approaching the garden from the standpoint of reversing what occurred at the Fall in Eden. In Eden at the Fall, the Divine Masculine and Feminine were separated, in Klingsor's Garden Wagner is going to reverse the curse.

Because Mary Magdalene was the first sent to herald the message of the resurrected Christ, in early Church history she was called, *Apostola Apostolorum*, *"the Apostle of the Apostles"*[35].

In this Sacred Stage Drama, Wagner also has masculine and feminine counterparts to reveal the Divine. Returning back to Gurnemanz's retelling of the Spear and Grail being given to Titurel, we find that the Spear and Grail represent those masculine and feminine counterparts. They are given to Titurel to be a *"treasured witness"*, Gurnemanz's wording, to a humanity of Divine Compassion.

"PARSIFAL: THE WILL AND REDEMPTION"

Symbolically, the Spear is a male phallic symbol representing the *Will-to-Give*. The Grail on the other hand, is the feminine counterpart, representing the *Will-to-Receive*. Together they reveal the qualities that unveil the Divine. In their union, the eternal creative force in both the spiritual realm and nature are made manifest. Thus, creation occurs in all dimensions, spiritual and natural. There is balance in those forces giving, receiving and giving back again, forming a cycle of eternal life. The balance of those forces gives peace, tranquility and rest to all dimensions of the spirit realm, and of nature.

This meaning of the Spear and Grail transcends their individual religious roots - Christian, Buddhist, pagan and even Jewish Mysticism, Kabbalah - and hence appears to unite them in a universal truth and revelation of the Divine. *This is why Genesis, for example, uses concepts and Names of God, which represent the Divine as being both Masculine and Feminine.* A feminine aspect of God in scripture is the *Holy Spirit*. Wherever the phrase רוּחַ הַקֹּדֶשׁ (Ruach HaKodesh, which is Hebrew for *Holy Spirit)* appears in the Old Testament it's always in the feminine. Thus, the Christian Trinity is made up of, the Father (Masculine), the Spirit (Feminine) and the Son. When this feminine attribute of the Spirit is first revealed in the New Testament, *she comes as a dove.* For the Son to be complete in fulfilling the revelation of the Divine, He also must have a feminine counterpart; thus, from His side issued forth His Bride, the Church. This is why in *Genesis* God creates male and female in His likeness, to depict the Divine attributes of Masculine and Feminine. In *Parsifal*, this is communicated through action, and through stage direction[36] regarding the Spear and the Grail when Parsifal and Kundry are reunited at the conclusion of Act III.

Gurnemanz tells us that something terrible has happened:

GURNEMANZ

O wondrous-wounding hallowed Spear! I saw thee wielded by unhallowed hand!

(absorbed in recollection)

All too bold Amfortas, thus armed, who could have prevented you from vanquishing the sorcerer? - Close to the castle our hero was drawn away: a woman of fearsome beauty enchanted him; in her arms he lay intoxicated, letting fall the Spear. A deathly cry! I rushed in: Klingsor, laughing, vanishing from there, having stolen the Holy Spear. Fighting, I garnered the king's flight; but a wound burned in his side; this wound which never heals.

The Holy Spear, representing *the Will-to-Give,* a Divine quality, was being wielded by unholy hands, so it is tempting (and common) to conclude that Klingsor must be the one of whom Gurnemanz spoke. However, it could also be that Klingsor obtained the Spear *because* it was in unholy hands; before Amfortas ever left Monsalvat he compromised himself and the Spear, long before he fell into the arms of Kundry, and before Klingsor took it from him. Amfortas was never commissioned by the Grail to vanquish Klingsor, and the Holy Spear was intended never to be used as a tool of violence, greed or selfish ambition regardless of how pious the cause. But Amfortas did take the Spear, which is a holy object that represents compassion and giving, to do just the opposite. Much of this is revealed as the drama continues.

The squires were amazed that Gurnemanz knew Klingsor and they enquired of him. So Gurnemanz continued telling the story *of "... the Savior's angel messengers ..."* who came down and gave Titurel the sacred vessel and Spear to be a witness to humanity. Titurel, though subtle as it may seem, focused on the *treasured* part, rather than their purpose as a *witness.* Remember, Wagner told us already he didn't care for the aspect of Hinduism that created a caste system, or the similar area in Buddhism. Here, Titurel is about to do the same thing by creating a shrine, a sanctuary and a special band of knights to protect the relics. Thus, what should have been treasured as a *living witness* was turned into *treasure* worthy of religious protection.

> GURNEMANZ
> For these relics he built a sanctuary. Others came to serve with him, taking paths no sinner can traverse, the pure alone, you know, can pass. These brethren the Grail gave miraculous strength.

There are two powerful statements made here - *"... taking paths no sinner can traverse ..."*, and *"... the Grail gave miraculous strength ..."*. The key to this inner drama is about the path to and from the domain of the Grail. *It's about the journey.* Sadly, if a sinner can't find the path, what's the point of the Grail and the Spear? Everything they represent is about sinners finding salvation. But as we will see as the drama unfolds, something has gone wrong with the direction Titurel has gone. However, for our young forthcoming hero, he is a sinner, and knows and says so himself, yet he finds the path and brings healing to all.

This is about transformation; we encounter obstacles and opportunities in life that help us transform. Depending on our response, the path is illuminated, or remains obscure. In a sense, the Grail is always calling; it sends us both obstacles and opportunities, while nudging us towards inner peace and sanctuary. Wagner is telling us that our goal should not be only about doing good deeds and avoiding evil ones, but about something far greater; this has taken Kundry's many lifetimes to grasp. When the squires questioned Kundry, prior to the explanation of the Spear and Grail, Gurnemanz said:

> GURNEMANZ
> She lives here now - perhaps anew to atone a debt from an earlier life not yet forgiven there.

In one sentence Wagner combines his point of view of Christianity and Buddhism into a single reality. Kundry is a reincarnation and she has come far in her journey. As a matter of fact, Gurnemanz explains that Titurel knew of her long before he ever built the Grail sanctuary.

GURNEMANZ
Titurel ... found her asleep in the undergrowth in the wood, numb, lifeless, as if dead. So I myself again found her shortly after we suffered that misfortune which that evildoer beyond the mountains brought upon us in such shame.

It is interesting that everyone, it seems, including Klingsor and Kundry start their journey in the meadow of the Grail. It wasn't as if they started out as being base people, or as being in a demonic place; nor did they start evil and have to work their way back to some level of divinity. Rather it all started there in the meadows of the sanctuary. Remember, supposedly, "... *paths no sinner can traverse, the pure alone ... can pass ...*". So how is it that a supposed sinner like Kundry or the wounded Amfortas can be there? How can the dull squires be in such a place? How can you and I, as observers, be there?

Nonetheless, awakening from slumber, like Kundry and even the squires, with their respective choices, seem to determine where the path leads. Since there are many lifetimes involved, *the path awoken to today has much to do with the passages traveled before.*

Compared to what the Christian and Buddhist religion evolved into, Wagner's characters are shedding their dogmatic religious shells, to reveal their inner, hidden spiritual truth.

For Wagner, Art is the deliverer of true spirituality, in contrast to traditional religion which creates a false sense of piety, a self-centered opinion of being on the correct path, and an illusion of what reality appears to be from Divine and natural perspectives. In its simplest expression, because I think I am right, God has to be on my side. This was the position of Amfortas as he took the Spear and sought out Klingsor. After all, according to Gurnemanz, *"... the Grail gave miraculous strength ..."* to those who walked the path. Unfortunately for Amfortas, he took and then misused the Spear for his own egoistic (religious) purposes and didn't recognize what the Spear truly was. Thus, before he even got past the sanctuary doors he was already wielding it with 'unholy hands'.

From the point of view of the Hindu and Buddhist religions, Kundry is doomed to reincarnate in the required lower caste until she corrects her wrongs from both present and past lives. In the same manner, Klingsor is also doomed to the caste of the base realm he occupies until he corrects his past wrongs:

GURNEMANZ
Therefore it was forbidden Klingsor, of whom you ask, though he made every effort. Yonder in the valley he lived secluded, beyond lies a rich heathen land. I never knew what sin he was guilty there, but then he wished to atone and indeed become sanctified. Powerless to stifle the sin within him, on himself he laid dastardly hands, which he then turned toward the Grail and by its guardian he was turned away. Thereupon the rage now instructed Klingsor how his deed of shameful sacrifice could give him council of evil magic; this he now found. He transformed the desert into a magic garden in which bloomed women of infernal beauty; there he awaits the knights of the Grail to lure them to sinful joys and hell's damnation: he gains control of those he entices; full many of us has he ruined. When Titurel, much burdened with age, had conferred sovereignty on his son, Amfortas could not wait to subdue this plague of sorcery. You know what happened there; the spear is now in Klingsor's hands:

if he can wound even a holy man with it, he fancies the Grail already firmly his!

Klingsor started in the realm of the Grail but had some sinful problem. Due to the nature of the drama and in particular its use of sexuality, the suggestion is that Klingsor had a lust problem and eventually emasculated himself, becoming a eunuch. This caused him to be rejected from the realm of the Grail. A reference usually referred to is Wagner's statement in *Hero-dom and Christendom:*

> *"It was a weighty feature of the Christian Church, that none but sound and healthy persons were admitted to the vow of total world-renunciation; and bodily defect, not to say mutilation, unfitted them."*[37]

The Catholic and sects of the Protestant Church, from Old Testament source text, precluded men from serving in the priesthood if they had such defects.

> *"He who is emasculated by crushing or mutilation shall not enter the assembly of the Lord."*[38]

> *"And the Lord spoke to Moses, saying, 'Speak to Aaron', saying: 'No man of your descendants in succeeding generations, who has any defect, may approach to offer the bread of his God. For any man who has a defect shall not approach: a man blind or lame, who has a marred face ... or is a eunuch.'"*[39]

However, in the New Testament, in the teachings of Christ and His Apostles, we find the opposite. On the issue of being emasculated:

> *"Now an angel of the Lord spoke to Philip, saying, 'rise and go toward the south along the road which goes down from Jerusalem to Gaza.' This is desert. So he arose and went. And behold, a man of Ethiopia, a eunuch of great authority under Candace the queen of the Ethiopians, who had charge of all her treasury, and had come to Jerusalem to worship, was*

returning. And sitting in his chariot, he was reading Isaiah the prophet. Then the Spirit said to Philip, 'Go near and overtake this chariot'. So Philip ran to him, and heard him reading the prophet Isaiah, and said, 'Do you understand what you are reading?' And he said, 'How can I, unless someone guides me?' And he asked Philip to come up and sit with him. ... So the eunuch answered Philip and said, 'I ask you, of whom does the prophet say this, of himself or of some other man?' Then Philip opened his mouth, and beginning at this Scripture, preached Jesus to him. Now as they went down the road, they came to some water. And the eunuch said, 'See, here is water. What hinders me from being baptized?' Then Philip said, 'If you believe with all your heart, you may'. And he answered and said, 'I believe that Jesus Christ is the Son of God'. So he commanded the chariot to stand still. And both Philip and the eunuch went down into the water, and he baptized him."[40]

In the Old Testament (or Torah), *Deuteronomy* and *Leviticus* describe restrictions pertaining to eunuchs; they are not permitted to come into the presence of God or to serve as a priest. But through the leadership of the Holy Spirit and what the Christ accomplished, Philip, a good Jewish boy who knew the Torah, is led to fellowship with an Ethiopian eunuch. Philip then baptizes him into God's presence. It wasn't that Philip was being defiant; it was that the work of Christ on the Cross, the shedding of His blood and the resurrected Life He offers, usurps the written code. Sadly, the Church has reinstituted a rule that was abolished in Christ. This is one of the implications that Wagner notes regarding the Church saying, *"... if Christianity had already been a living part of it, the Church has utterly destroyed it."*

Interpreted literally, it appears that Jesus is telling His disciples to do what Klingsor did:

"If your hand or foot causes you to sin, cut it off and cast it from you. It is better for you to enter into life lame or maimed, rather than having two hands or two feet, to be cast into the everlasting fire."[41]

However, in context, Jesus is speaking metaphorically to make a spiritual point; he wasn't condoning self-mutilation as religious practice. Yet, there are those in the world of Christendom who have taken these verses out of context, practicing such things as worshiping with poisonous snakes, or self-flagellation to prove their piety. In our Sacred Stage Drama, Klingsor was prevented from entering the brotherhood of the Grail, not by the Grail itself, but according to Gurnemanz, by its *guardian, Titurel!* Here again *religion shrouds Divine certainty*. According to Gurnemanz, Klingsor tried to atone for his sinfulness, but Titurel would not accept it. How horrible is this! The Spear and Grail represent atonement through Christ's display of *Free-Will-Suffering*, yet, Klingsor is led to believe he must atone for his sinfulness. In Christian theology, Christ already atoned for Klingsor's sinfulness and for that of the world, but Titurel is not allowing that to Klingsor. Titurel has lost the meaning of the Grail and Spear in his effort to protect them. More on this later. For Klingsor there is nothing left; there is no way to pay the debt, so he leaves in despair. Klingsor loses faith and replaces it with humanistic belief in Enlightenment. Now, acquiring the relics is to support his superiority over them, not to admire and revere them. Keep in mind, he was not rejected from the Divine itself; rather it was the traditional religious system of Titurel that rejected him, which was supposedly protecting the Grail.

Klingsor, Kundry and Amfortas are all in pain, for different reasons; yet all are encompassed by the same caste and legalistic system. The knights and squires are oblivious; they recognize Amfortas is suffering, and they tend to him not because of compassion but because he has the duty to unveil the Grail. Their need to be the brotherhood of the Grail, which gives them strength is more important than he who suffers. Amfortas to them is a means to an end. They recognize Kundry as a base creature, though she serves them tirelessly. They see her as the bringer of trouble when she is among them; they ridicule her and mock her. She is never accepted by them. She can't be because she is of lower class. Actually, when she is in the realm of the Grail, things stay in order, it is when she leaves for long periods that bad things happen:

> GURNEMANZ
> Yes, when she stays afar too long misfortune then befalls us.

What if there wasn't the caste system and religiosity among the knights? Would Kundry find acceptance, peace and resolve?

The knights and squires see Klingsor to be a heinous being. Full of the devil and all that is evil, they see him as the source of their plight. If he didn't exist, they would have no need to fight against the injustice that befalls others, because in their mind Klingsor is responsible. At this point, he possesses the sacred Spear, which is the gnawing mark of their hindrance to perfection. To have it back would mean total victory! If it wasn't for Klingsor they wouldn't be losing fellow knights to the she-devils that he created as weapons. They wouldn't have to constantly bathe their ailing Amfortas, who is a victim in their minds of Klingsor's evil doing.

Can you hear the religious pride in all of this? Once we enter the sanctuary, the knights desire to go forth and fight for their brotherhood and do good deeds in the name of the Grail. But in their reality where their truth abides, their sense of religious piety depends on striving to overcome a Klingsor. If there was no Klingsor, with his dark castle guarded by the she-devils of moral destruction, and he was just a chef in the kitchen of Monsalvat; they would have no purpose. Their religious system requires a Klingsor to give them a sense of godliness and resolution. They need to perceive evil, to make themselves feel good. They need to accuse Klingsor, so they can feel righteous. It was Titurel that banished Klingsor because he struggled to reach the unattainable standard set by Titurel's religiosity. The Grail never set such a standard. Their religious system created the enemy, so they could feel righteous about themselves. In contrast we will see, it is through both the journey and through communing with the Grail that one's full divine potential is realized:

> 4th SQUIRE
> Above all else; the Spear must be returned!
>
> 3rd SQUIRE
> Ha! He who brought it back will have fame and fortune!

Once again, the egoistic rant of their religion speaks, *"... he who brought it [the Spear] back will have fame and fortune!"* This of course has nothing to do with the reality of what is holy and true as far as both Spear and Grail are concerned. Because of all this religious illusion of spirituality, which shrouds the true Spirit, there is great suffering.

Furthermore, there is one who is suffering that transcends all of the brotherhood, including Titurel, Amfortas, Kundry and even Klingsor. There is one who is suffering in the sanctuary of the Grail, who has not yet been revealed.

Gurnemanz concludes his story of Titurel, Klingsor and Amfortas, by revealing the one hope given to them from Heaven:

> GURNEMANZ
> Before the looted sanctuary Amfortas lay in fervent prayer, anxiously imploring some sign of salvation: a blessed radiance emanated from the Grail; a holy vision clearly spoke to him this message in words of fire: "Enlightened through compassion, the innocent fool; wait for him, the appointed one".
>
> FOUR SQUIRES
> *(deeply moved)*

"PARSIFAL: THE WILL AND REDEMPTION"

Enlightened through compassion, the innocent fool ...

(From the lake are heard shouts and cries from the knights and squires. Gurnemanz and the four squires get up and turn with great alarm.)

KNIGHTS AND SQUIRES
Alas! Alas! Hoho! Up! Who is the scoundrel!

(A wild swan flutters in tangled flight from the lake. He's wounded. The squires and knights follow. The swan falls to the ground after a difficult flight. The second knight draws an arrow from its chest.)

The swan in the European myths had many usages, but the most central was of it being a *shape shifter.* It would transform from swan to human when necessary. Throughout the Teutonic and Germanic legends, we see swans in very significant moments. In the last chapter, we pointed out that Wagner in *Lohengrin* used a swan to transform into Gottfried. Ortrud turned Gottfried into the swan, and Lohengrin through prayer, transformed him back into human form.

The swan begins its life as rather ordinary, or as in the famous fairy tale by Hans Christian Anderson, an ugly duckling.[42] But as it matures it is transformed into a beautiful, large winged creature.

In our Sacred Stage Drama, the swan is a spiritual being yet to be incarnated, or reincarnated. It was flying, as if from the heavenly worlds and is struck by an arrow and flutters to the lower world of time, space and matter. No sooner does it 'fall' to the ground, a young totally ignorant youth appears; he doesn't even know his own name.

Because our nameless youth is a reincarnation of Siegfried, we can learn from Siegfried why he enters the Grail's domain in this manner. Siegfried, the naïve fearless hero, who learns fear from Brünnhilde, has one quality that keeps him from progressing - unrestrained violence. From choking Mime in the first act of *Siegfried*, too wresting the ring back from Brünnhilde while under the influence of a potion in *Götterdämmerung,* this is his flaw. Therefore, we have a youth whose issue is violence.

His mindless violence weighs down his 'higher' self as the swan, and so he enters the 'lower' world. We see violence again when Kundry tells him about his mother's death: he springs forth and chokes her. And, just as our youth wounded the swan, who else do we know who was similarly wounded - Amfortas! And who struck Amfortas, but Klingsor. Consequently, when our youth confronts Klingsor, it's as if he's confronting a part of himself. Will the youth respond by violence again? We will see ...

The knights claim Amfortas saw the swan as a happy omen until the arrow struck it. They present the youth; the squires want vengeance. Gurnemanz is puzzled and declares it to be an unprecedented act. He speaks to the youth, explaining how all the animals in this land are friendly and kind. Then Gurnemanz lets us in on a secret that to many would pass us by:

GURNEMANZ
Seeking his mate, he flew up to circle with it over the lake and gloriously to dedicate the bath.

Isn't this what the story is all about? The reuniting of the Spear and Grail? The reuniting of the *Will-to-Give* and the *Will-to-Receive?* The reuniting of the Divine Masculine and Feminine? If they were united, the swan and its mate, Gurnemanz says that it would have gloriously dedicated the bath. If the bath was dedicated to and by Divine revelation, then Amfortas would have been healed. But, such union did not occur. Here the swan rose to the highest of the spiritual worlds seeking its mate but was met with an arrow through its chest. The masculine and feminine attributes of the Divine are still separated in the lower world. But if that be the case, then who is this youth, in this incarnation?

"PARSIFAL: THE WILL AND REDEMPTION"

P ART 2: Religion Threatened By Foolishness

A swan has fallen to the lower world. It is pierced by an arrow and materializes in human form. Who is it? *The swan is the very youth who shot it.* This may sound like a contradiction, but it is a central, key concept that speaks to transformation and redemption in the drama. Much of Wagner's prose works were proving grounds for his music dramas, like the famous dialogue between Wotan and Fricka in Act II of *Die Walküre* which was originally forged in *Jesus of Nazareth*. In the same manner, many of the spiritual concepts in *Parsifal* come directly from the same work:

> "... *God is love, and of love he sent to you his son; whose brothers all men are, and like unto him through love.' Every creature loves, and Love is the law of select for all creation; so if Man made a law to shackle love, to reach a goal that lies outside of human nature (namely, power, dominion - above all: the protection of property) he sinned against the law of his own existence, and therewith slew himself; but in that we acknowledge Love, and vindicate it from the law of the false spirit, we raise ourselves above the brute creation, since we arrive at knowledge of the everlasting law which has been the sole power from the ur-beginning; ... and thus are co-creators with God at every moment, and through the consciousness of*

that are God himself. Jesus knows and practices God's-love through his teaching of it in a consciousness of Cause and Effect: he accordingly is God and the Son of God; but every man is capable of like knowledge and like practice, - and if he attain thereto, he is like unto God and Jesus." [43]

As in the meadows of the Grail, every creature is in a Divine state of love. Gurnemanz asks the youth:

GURNEMANZ
Did not the animals tamely greet you, friendly and pious?

Wagner writes:

"... so if a Man made a law to shackle love, to reach a goal that lies outside of human nature (namely, power, dominion - above all: the protection of property) he sinned against the law of his own existence, and therewith slew himself ..."

The nameless youth is a reincarnation of a past life, Siegfried. Siegfried bore Wotan's curse, and so betrayed his love, Brünnhilde, and through that he awakened her and she became a woman of wisdom:

BRÜNNHILDE
... you sacrificed him who wrought it to the curse which had fallen on you: this innocent had to betray me so that I should become a woman of wisdom!
(Gotterdammerung: Act III, Scene 3)

Kundry, the reincarnation of Brünnhilde, knows more than others in the drama because in the last moments of her previous life her soul became wise in the person of Brünnhilde. Yet she still has to reconcile the wound that she brings into her current life as Kundry. Our nameless youth has all the attributes of Siegfried; ignorance, innocence, and violence, but *he also was a traitor to his feminine counterpart.* In addition, in the beginning of the third act of

Götterdämmerung, he refused to give the Ring back to the Rhinemaidens. Thus, the curse of Wotan has taken its toll; *Siegfried was now protecting his property:*

SIEGFRIED
My sword shattered a spear: even if they wove wild curses into it, Nothung will sever for the Norns' the eternal rope of primeval law! A dragon indeed once warned me of the curse, but did not teach me to fear it!

(He gazes at the ring)

A ring would win me the world's wealth: for the gift of love I gladly relinquish it: I would give it to you if you granted me love. But by threatening life and limb, be it by less than a finger's worth, you will not wrest the ring from me! For life and limb, see - thus I fling them from me!

(Gotterdammerung: Act III, Scene 1)

There is much that could be said about this segment of Siegfried's dialogue, however, he's protecting his property. The Ring in and of itself was never the god's real problem. Wotan, the gods and Valhalla were simply a reflection of the other side of the same mirror as Alberich, the dwarves and Nibelheim. The only difference between Wotan and Alberich, is what they gave to obtain what they gained. Yet in the end, they both lost what was most precious to them.

While the author has avoided discussion of leitmotifs, which are extensively treated in the existing *Ring* literature, one is compelled to mention that the leitmotif of Valhalla is the same as that of the Ring, with only minor variation.[44] Thus, Wotan needed no Ring forged by Alberich to be a victim of a curse that seeks world domination and forswears love. Wotan forged Valhalla in the same manner that Alberich forged the Ring, with cunning, deceit and thievery. This is what Siegfried became, and what an unwitting Brünnhilde helped confer on him. It wasn't until the conclusion of

Götterdämmerung through Siegfried's betrayal, that Brünnhilde realized what had happened. She now became a woman of wisdom. The only way to bring this dilemma to a conclusion was to return the Ring from whence it came, and to set in motion a cleansing of Siegfried from both the curse of Valhalla and the curse of the Ring. She did this by giving the only thing that could set this in motion; the ultimate expression of Love which defies all that tries to shackle it, the selfish *Will-to-Receive-for-Itself*. Thus, Brünnhilde gave *herself;* she gave up her *Will-to-Live* for the *Will-to-Love.*

The process has now been set in motion. The gallant Valkyrie in the world of the Ring is the lowest of all those in the caste system of Monsalvat. The nameless youth, like a child born into a new world, the reincarnated Siegfried, enters just as bold and ignorant as before. Wagner said, *"... but in that we acknowledge Love, and vindicate it from the law of the false spirit, we raise ourselves above the brute creation, since we arrive at the knowledge of the everlasting law which has been the sole power from the ur-beginning ...."*

The swan with the arrow through its breast is that which slew itself, the nameless youth. It falls from the higher spiritual world back to the lower world of *brute creation.* It can't abide in the higher worlds, because the process of transformation and attainment of divinity has yet to be fulfilled. What has been set in motion is now realized as Kundry and Parsifal. That which was Gottfried, then Siegfried, is now the nameless youth, Parsifal.

The youth seems to know nothing except his origins. He can recollect his mother, Herzeleide *(Heart's Sorrow),* and that they lived in the woods. He explains to Gurnemanz that he made the bow himself to keep away savage eagles from their home. As they discuss his weapon, Kundry (the one who is *knowing),* breaks into the conversation:

KUNDRY
His mother bore him fatherless, for Gamuret was slain in battle! To preserve her son from a similar untimely hero's death, she reared him up in the desert to folly, a stranger to arms - the fool!

The reflections of the youth's previous life appear. Like Siegfried before him, whose father Siegmund was slain in battle, his father Gamuret was slain in similar fashion, so he too was born fatherless. They both grew up in the forest, and the weapons they donned were used to kill wild beasts. But then he was attracted to the forest's edge and the civilization that lay beyond. He met gallant knights and desired to be like them, but they arrogantly laughed at him and rode off. He tried to overtake them but failed. He tells Gurnemanz and Kundry that he traveled far and wide, met many wild beasts and giants with only his bow to defend himself.

In Buddhism, the bow and arrow are significant. The bow represents *wisdom* and the arrow represents *method*.[45] Evidently the youth has wisdom because of his inner innocence, it is just that his method hasn't been developed with proper focus. For the youth, the only method he knows is violence. To develop the proper method, we need to resolve that which keeps us from connecting to a higher realm; the realm from which the swan fell - the realm of the Divine:

KUNDRY
Yes! Robbers and giants engaged his strength: they learned to fear the fierce boy.

PARSIFAL
(surprised)

Who fears me? Say!

KUNDRY
The wicked!

PARSIFAL
They who threatened me, were they wicked?

(Gurnemanz laughs)

Who is good?

The youth's ignorance goes beyond not knowing his name or the details of his life; he also cannot distinguish between Divine Life (symbolized by the Tree of Life), and Spiritual Death (symbolized by the Tree of the Knowledge of Good and Evil). Wagner held that the greatest of this lower world's deceptions is traditional religion; and of this deception our nameless youth is ignorant. The youth asked, *"... were they wicked? Who is good?"* What, then is Spiritual Death? Spiritual Death in metaphor is the world of time and matter; it is that which shuts one's eyes to Divine reality. It is not ceasing to exist, but the inability to perceive and/or reveal the Divine.

Wagner will bring us into the garden of Spiritual Death in the second act where he makes comparisons to the first three chapters of the book of *Genesis*:

> *"And out of the ground the Lord God made every tree to grow that is pleasant to the sight and good for food. The tree of life was also in the midst of the garden, and the tree of the knowledge of good and evil. ... And the Lord God commanded the man, saying, 'Of every tree of the garden you may freely eat; but of the tree of the knowledge of good and evil you shall not eat, for in the day that you eat of it you shall surely die."* [46]

In the book of *Genesis* we are told there are two trees in The Garden - the Tree of Life, and the Tree of the Knowledge of Good and Evil. The choice set before us is either Divinity, the Tree of Life; or selfish ambition, the making of ourselves as a god, the Tree of the Knowledge of Good and Evil. Wagner specifically says in *Parsifal* that the Divine prophecy to Amfortas is *"Enlightened through compassion ..."*, and not *"Enlightened through knowing good from evil"*. This is what makes the nameless youth appear to be a fool - he doesn't

"PARSIFAL: THE WILL AND REDEMPTION"

know good from evil. The issue is, in which direction is the arrow pointed? By which *method* is the youth going to learn - from the Tree of Life; or from what Wagner might call the Tree of Death, the *Knowledge of Good and Evil?* Because he has yet to learn, as it were from which tree he will partake, he asks Kundry who is it that fears him. She replies, *"The wicked!"*. Even from his 'ignorant' perspective of the Knowledge of Good and Evil, he still has the potential to partake of Life, the key to which as per Wagner is *Divine compassion.* Thus he is dangerous to the wicked who rule in a Realm of Death, the Knowledge of Good and Evil.

No sooner does he ask the question of who is good, Gurnemanz attempts to provide him with a point of reference. By relating to Parsifal from a good-and-evil standpoint, notice the suggestion of guilt that Gurnemanz offers the youth:

> GURNEMANZ
> Your mother, whom you deserted and who now worries and grieves for you.

No sooner does the nameless youth arrive in this world, does its system attempt to assign him to the social order of the Knowing of Good and Evil:

> KUNDRY
> She grieves no more: his mother is dead.

> PARSIFAL
> *(in fearful alarm)*
> Dead? My mother? Who says so?

> KUNDRY
> As I rode by I saw her dying: she entreated me to give the fool her greeting.

> *(Parsifal leaps at Kundry and seizes her by the throat. Gurnemanz restrains him.)*

> GURNEMANZ
> Insane youth? Again violent?

(After Gurnemanz has freed Kundry, Parsifal stands as if dazed, seized with violent trembling)

What has the woman done to you? She spoke the truth; Kundry never lies, though she has seen much.

PARSIFAL
I am fainting!

While Kundry spoke correctly, she provided no compassion; she instigated a reaction of shock and violence. But then isn't this once again the focal point of the drama - the masculine and feminine qualities of the Divine being united? However, in the lower world of time and matter, they are still separate. These two characters are destined to be made one, but at this point are still separate - not spatially, but spiritually. They are blind to each other's worldviews and so in this lower, fallen world are at odds.

Reminding ourselves of what we discussed in Part 1; Kundry is trapped by the dogma of deeds for salvation: the Tree of the Knowledge of Good and Evil. She's trapped by traditional religion and can't escape. She works towards acceptance and absolution from the system, but can't break out of its grip. She's totally exhausted. *She can't do enough to be good enough.* She wants nothing more than to rest, to sleep. But when she does rest, her base nature takes over. She has no spiritual potency to raise her to a higher level, to overcome her base nature. As per Wagner, there is no Divinity in traditional religion: "*... in that we acknowledge Love, and vindicate it from the law of the false spirit, we raise ourselves above the brute creation ...*". Kundry is still bound by the *law of the false spirit;* she is still bound by the *brute creation:*

GURNEMANZ
Well done, according to the Grail's mercy: they vanquish evil who requite it with good.

KUNDRY
I never do good; I long only for rest ...

"PARSIFAL: THE WILL AND REDEMPTION"

(while Gurnemanz tends Parsifal in a fatherly way, she creeps unobserved by them towards a thicket in the wood)

... only rest in my weariness. To sleep! O that no one would wake me!

(starting in fear)

No! Not sleep! Horror seizes me!

(She falls into a violent trembling, then lets her arms and head drop wearily and totters away)

In vain to resist! The time has come. -

(By the lake a movement is seen, and at length in the background the train of knights and squires returning home with the litter.)

Sleep - sleep - I must.

(She sinks down behind the bushes and is not seen further.)

As Kundry disappears to the lowest brute force, Amfortas and the knights are returning from his bath. They prepare for worship. Gurnemanz invites the youth to observe; he explains that if he is pure the Grail will provide sustenance for him:

> PARSIFAL
> Who is the Grail?

He doesn't ask *what*, he asks *who*. Wagner begins the process of removing the symbolism to unmask the Divine reality which has been kept hidden. The Grail isn't a cup, it's a persona or representation of the Divine. But as we stated earlier, the Spear and the Grail are masculine and feminine qualities. So which is the Grail? It is that persona of the Divine Feminine:

GURNEMANZ
That cannot be said; but if you yourself are called to its service that knowledge will not remain withheld. - And see! I think I know you aright; no earthly path leads to it, and none could tread it whom the Grail itself had not guided:

PARSIFAL
I scarcely tread, yet seem already to have come far.

GURNEMANZ

You see, my son, time here becomes space.

"PARSIFAL: THE WILL AND REDEMPTION"

Part 3: Religion in the Inner World

Time becomes space. What a statement! In Wagner's day when these words were written, now well over a century ago, the Theory of Special Relativity was but a twinkle in Albert Einstein's parents' eyes, and the science of Quantum Mechanics was embryonic. Yet, these emergent concepts were not necessarily strange either, because they did not wholly originate in modern science; their spiritual, theological, and philosophical origins are ancient. Wagner employed what has become scientific assertion in the 21st Century, but there were glimmerings in early Christian and Eastern thought, and even in Kabbalah which said to date back to the *Zohar* in the 2nd Century AD. Still earlier origins may go back as far as the Babylonian exile over 2,600 years ago. So, in Wagner's view, as well as in Christianity, Buddhism and Kabbalah, the infinite spiritual world of inner consciousness, the distinction between time and space simply do not exist. Rather, within that dimension there are living spiritual expressions and qualities. Thus the Realm of the Grail has no material correlation whatsoever to the world of time and space, except to say they become one. (The only exception here is that Wagner is relating those ethereal realities on a physical stage, which is no easy task, and many times is interpretively misunderstood.) Thus, to relate the reality of that spiritual realm to a physical observing audience, Wagner has

Gurnemanz state that *time becomes space*. Thus, approaching the Castle of the Grail, we enter a timeless place were spiritual qualities extend past the physical world of the five senses. As one listens to and is carried by the forthcoming *Verwandlungsmusik (Transformation Music)* these concepts come alive. They are a collective union occupying a common space, whether in a state of rest or strain, or of elated tranquility or deep conflict. In many ways, the spiritual condition of that dimension is ebbing and flowing through these multiple states simultaneously revealing the ultimate intent of the Divine from which it emanates.

In the place where *time becomes space,* Wagner departs significantly from the writings of Arthur Schopenhauer, the roots of whose philosophy are expressed in his classic seminal work, *The World as Will and Representation*.[47] As a sweeping and grossly over-simplified summary, Schopenhauer's key concept is that each of us has a *Will*, and that one's recognition or perception of one's self, all of humanity, and the world is an expression or a representation of that *Will*. Wagner does not wholly disagree with that assumption, but he also does not entirely agree with it either. In *Parsifal* and many of his other operas, Wagner attempts to communicate what he believes to be sacred, unshakeable truths, and to resolve the problems he sees in the Schopenhauer's, as well as Nietzsche's, thinking.

Ironically, as noted above, concepts raised in *Parsifal* have spiritual connections to early Christian theology, Buddhism and Kabbalah. Whereas Schopenhauer and Nietzsche departed from spirituality, explaining human activity in terms only of a collective human *Will*, Wagner reengaged elemental aspects of spirituality and Divinity. He asserted their value and reality, departing from traditional religiosity and from the views of his philosophical contemporaries. Unlike Nietzsche, Wagner did not assert that there is no God, or that God is dead. Rather for him the Divine was alive, but not in a traditional Western Greco-Roman-

"PARSIFAL: THE WILL AND REDEMPTION"

Nordic sense, which he expressed in the burning of Valhalla. Wagner saw the collective *Will* of Schopenhauer as the Infinite Divine Creator of all things. To Wagner, the *Will* had meaning, but was not to him an intangible, or a fabrication of primitive man's need to calm his fears. Wagner's primary conceptualization of Schopenhauer's collective *Will* was as a *Will-to-Live*, a drive to survive existence. Further, Wagner considered the *Will* to be solely egoistic, which he called a *Will-to-Receive-only-for-Itself*. Hence, he restored the Divine to his philosophy, where Schopenhauer and Nietzsche removed it. Schopenhauer saw compassion as the key to the *Will* and to the development of humanity, on which point he and Wagner agreed. It was this that encouraged Wagner to study and find acceptable much of Schopenhauer's philosophy. However, for Wagner compassion wasn't a human trait in and of itself; he believed humans lived by their five senses and by the cravings of their egoistic flesh, or as Wagner calls it their *brute nature.*

For Wagner, the five senses and the egoistic flesh had to be overpowered by a higher world, a higher consciousness. For Wagner, who believed that Jesus was Divine, the image of Christ on the Cross was the greatest manifestation of *Free-Will-Suffering*. To him, *Free-Will-Suffering*, was central to how human beings discover true compassion without egoistic influence. In other words, the *brute nature* of man can claim to have compassion, but in reality that compassion still retains elements of self-interest. Consider a person feeding the hungry; does he perform the deed selflessly, sincerely loving the one he feeds? Or, does he do it because it makes him feel better about himself? Often it is more the latter than the former, which with its elements of self-interest also often can involve self-deception.

In traditional religion, to use Wagner's terminology, man attempts to overpower his *brute nature* by 'serving God', rather than truly emulating the nature of God Himself. Rather, Wagner believed that to emulate God, one must return to true compassion, and to restrain egoistic intention, which in Christian terms is referred to as 'crucifixion of the flesh'. This is why Wagner commented to Constantin Franz that the way from man to God is through compassion, and His eternal name is *Jesus*. Wagner was not promoting a 'coming to Jesus' in a 1980's fundamentalist sense. In many cases he would see that no different than the traditional religion he was criticizing. While he would not object to the recognition of a 'coming to Jesus', he was more interested in emulating the Divine, than in adding more symbols, dogmas and labels.

Wagner was in many respects out on a limb in his views, an extreme evidence of which was Nietzsche's famous/infamous condemnation of Wagner's treatment of spirituality. In the Enlightenment perspective common to that era, it was common to attempt to explain human nature without including mention of God and religion, which were thought to be for the weak-minded and the non-thinking.

Wagner proclaims another path in *The Ring* and *Parsifal*. In thought and conviction, he tells us that God exists and that we are part of that Infinite Being's creative expression. The problem for Wagner wasn't in a belief in the Divine (i.e., God), or in the view that the collective *Will* was the Divine, but with humanity's concealment of Him through its expressions in traditional religion and equally, the removal of Him by those who claim Enlightenment and humanistic philosophy.

Thus Wagner created *Parsifal*, a Sacred Stage Drama to address those who remove the Divine from their thinking and as well, to free God from religion's ever growing heap of incredibilities that conceal Him.

To the traditional religious mind, only those who are truly holy and morally correct can connect to Divinity. The Keepers of the Grail are deluded in believing that they are serving the Grail because they have attained some form of purity, even though the edifice and system founded by their religious leader, Titurel, effectively conceals the Divine from those who desire that connection.

For the next twelve to fifteen minutes in Act I, some of Wagner's most beautiful music takes us on a journey known as the *Verwandlungsmusik* - Transformation Music. The music itself is arranged in such a way where leitmotif, tempo and chromatic structure give the impression of time giving way to space, and space to formlessness and then back to reformation. Within the period of the *Verwandlungsmusik*, there are five key changes as Wagner moves us through A^b, C, B^b, E^b, and then back to C. When we arrive back at C major, the powerful chimes of Monsalvat announce our arrival; we find ourselves in the Inner Sanctuary of the Grail.

The first set of bells that Wagner constructed in 1879 for Act I was a piano-like instrument that stood almost seven and a half feet tall (220 cm). The long, thick strings were struck by hammers over three inches wide.[48] By 1882, for the first performance of the opera, Wagner added a large hammer dulcimer constructed by the same company. He also added additional instruments for sound coloring like, tone barrels and tam-tams. The deep bass, again in the circle of fifths, C, G, A, E, had a percussive impact in the Festival house. According to the manufacturer, Steingraeber und Söhne, to create the low E bell in an actual cathedral tower, which would be twenty steps lower than the lowest bell at St. Stephen's Cathedral in Vienna, it would have had to have been constructed of cast iron over 26 feet (8 meters) in diameter, weighing 286 tons (260 tonnes). Sadly, Wagner was never happy with the outcome; his bells never created the percussive and tonal impact he wanted.

Upon entering the inner sanctuary to the accompaniment of the bells, into what is presumed in the World of the Grail to be the infinite world of the Divine, Gurnemanz tells the youth:

GURNEMANZ
Now watch and let me see, if you're a fool and innocent, what wisdom may be revealed to you.

Why a fool and innocent? The fool who is innocent lacks knowledge, and in the traditional religious mind, *and* paradoxically for believers in the Enlightenment, Knowledge is everything. For the traditional religious mind the Knowledge of Good and Evil is used to achieve union with God. For believers in the Enlightenment, that Knowledge reveals that there is no need for God. For Wagner, only the innocent fool can bypass these diversions.

The Grail knights and squires start filling the hall. They say some wonderful things affirming their religious delusion.

GRAIL KNIGHTS
...The meal will renew him who delights in doing good: may he find refreshment and receive the supreme gift.

Their delusion is in believing that this is true and valid. Once again we see how traditional religion can turn things upside down. In contrast to their religious beliefs, we hear a musical dramatic truth quietly heralded by wave upon wave of chorus voices from the dome above. Of course, like our youth observing, they too are voices of youth:

YOUTHS
As once His blood flowed with countless pains for the sinful world - the Redeeming Hero be it with a joyful heart my blood shed. His body, that He gave to purge our sin, lives in us through His death.

BOYS
Faith endures; the dove hovers, the Savior's loving messenger. Drink the wine poured out for you and take the Bread of Life.

As the voices climb to the apex of the dome, we see a difference between what is proclaimed from the unseen world, and from the world of the knights. The message of the voices is that the Savior shed His blood to bring redemption. The youth say, *"... be it with a joyful heart my blood shed"*. This has nothing to do with going against the Klingsors of the world and dying for the cause of their religion. But it has everything to do with dying for the *Self-Will*, the *Ego*, and the *Will-to-Live*, to become like the Savior who through compassion revealed the *Will-to-Redeem*. Wagner tells us:

> *"In the history of Christianity we certainly heed repeated instances of miraculous powers conferred by pure virginity ... the mystery of motherhood without natural impregnation can only be traced to the greater miracle, the birth of God himself: born into this the 'Denial-of-the-World' is revealed in a life prefiguratively offered up for its redemption. As the Savior Himself was recognized, sinless, nay, incapable of sin, it followed in Him that the Will must have been completely broken ere ever He was born so that He could no more suffer, but only feel for others' sufferings; and the root here was necessarily found in a birth that issued, not from the 'Will-to-Live', but from the 'Will-to-Redeem'."* [49]

Wagner stated *"...in Him that Will must have been completely broken ere ever, He was born so that He could no more suffer, but only feel for other's sufferings..."*. The *Will-to-Redeem* is born of *Free-Will-Suffering*. So, Wagner is saying that Jesus' *Will* (*Will-to-Live*, the *Will-to-Receive-for-Itself-Alone*, and *Egoism*) was broken before birth by Compassion, the *Will-to-Redeem*.

Although there are similarities, the context and usage of the word *Ego* here should not be related directly to the Ego of Freudian thought. Rather, both the author and Wagner use the word *Ego* more in a colloquial sense. Freud didn't start developing his concepts of Id, Ego and Super-Ego, until 1911, long after Wagner's death.

Wagner makes a distinction between pain and suffering. He does not deny human pain, but he tells us that the *Will-to-Live*, thus the *Ego*, is the cause of most human suffering. We suffer because our *Ego* doesn't want to be in the position it is in. For example, if the *Ego* does not like sitting on a hard chair, or does not like the emotional turbulence of serious financial problems, it suffers. When this *Egoism (i.e., the Will-to-Live)* is expunged, such things no longer cause suffering. They may still be painful, but they don't cause suffering. But just censoring/expunging the *Ego* isn't enough. Like the serpent in the Garden, the *Ego* is subtle and crafty. The *Ego* will endure suffering if it believes its outcome will be of benefit to itself.

Free-Will-Suffering, from which is born the *Will-to-Redeem*, is different. It doesn't have an *Ego* that does things for itself; rather it experiences suffering only because others suffer. Through perception, not mere belief, it has found true peace within itself through its revelation of Divinity. Thus the outgrowth of that connection is emulation of God, not works of service for acceptance; one does what he does because it is his nature - his Divine nature. The pathway to a Divine nature and expunging *Ego* is *Compassion*. The first revelation of this is when we realize the Divine has already revealed his compassion to us personally, as we will see in the second act. For us to become compassionate, which is a Divine quality, we must first allow compassion into our lives. It appears with Christ on the Cross where through His sacrifice, He atones for our sins, and thus we need not atone for ourselves.[50] In that statement, every aspect of the *brute nature*, the *Will-to-Live*, the *Ego*, the *Self-Will*, says, *"No! I can't accept that! I must atone for my own sins!"* This is where Nietzsche cries out, *"Weakness!"* [51] Thus for Nietzsche, to bow to the Christian Cross and to accept Divine atonement is weakness; we must rather find our own way, atone and grow for ourselves. To Wagner, in Christianity, Buddhism, and Kabbalah, to express the wide range of these spiritual concepts is nothing more

"PARSIFAL: THE WILL AND REDEMPTION"

than the *brute nature*, the *Self-Will*, trying to survive rather than to be transformed into something greater. It is Enlightenment arrogance, in effect trying to attain godliness without also attaining its essence.

These ideas are divergent from Schopenhauer and Nietzsche. Wagner said on December 1, 1858, that while complementing Schopenhauer's ideas, he also felt he needed to correct him:

"I then studied a good deal of philosophy and reached conclusions which complement and correct my friend Schopenhauer. But I prefer to contemplate on such matters than write them down. On the other hand, poetic projects are again crowding into my mind in a most lively fashion. Parzival has preoccupied me very much. In particular, there is an interesting creature, a strangely world-demonic woman who is the messenger of the grail, and who strikes me with increasing vitality and fascination."[52]

The venue through which this correction came is *Parsifal*. The idea of *compassion* and the *Will-to-Redeem* have little in common with Enlightenment. When love and kindness are spoken of in Enlightenment they still speak from a self-centered, egoistic perspective. In other words, I love or desire you because of how you make me feel. To put it yet another way, I love because of what I get out of it. Not here. Not for Wagner, nor in this drama.

Wagner wrote extensively on this topic, all of which is available in print. Wagner presents here a new *Will* in the Enlightenment equation. This is the restoration of the Divine intent of redemption in the human condition.

Wotan's Valhalla was created from the same intention, or *Will-to-Receive-for-Itself* as Alberich's Ring; similarly, Titurel says:

TITUREL

"EXPLORING RICHARD WAGNER'S FINAL TREATISE"

Amfortas, my son, are you in your place?

(long silence)

Shall I again today look on the Grail and live?

(long silence)

Must I die without my Savior's guidance?

The religious leader (Titurel) that excommunicated and thus in effect created the Klingsor that now threatens Monsalvat, now speaks. The definitive voice of the *Ego, Self-Will*, self-centeredness and religiosity speaks. There is no compassion for his suffering son, Amfortas. Rather he messages - *keep the religion alive! Let me live, even if you suffer to do so.* Like Wotan and his reciprocal Alberich, Titurel in selfishness desires to misuse the power of Divine Life, like his counterpart Klingsor. Klingsor desires to apprehend the Grail, whereas Titurel, desires to protect it. Remember Wagner's words: *"... (namely, power, dominion - above all: the protection of property), he sinned against the law of his own existence ...".* These are two sides of the same coin; one desires to apprehend the prize and hoard it, while the other hoards and protects it:

AMFORTAS
Woe! Woe is me! The agony! My father, oh, once perform the office. Live, live and let me die!

TITUREL
In the tomb I live by the Savior's grace. But I am too weak to serve Him. You can atone for your sin in His service. Uncover the Grail!

Once again the distortion of the religion that keeps Kundry helping (to no successful end) and Amfortas serving (in torment with no relief) proclaims the lie, *You can atone for your sin in His service.* But such a notion is a spiritual impossibility. Amfortas proclaims what religion does to humanity:

AMFORTAS
No! Leave it covered! Oh that nobody understand this torture that is awakened in me by what delights you!

Amfortas continues to disclose his horrific torture brought about by his wound and his religion's delight in its dismissal. The knights basically say to Amfortas that what's important is that he keep doing what gives *them* pleasure in spite of his suffering.

The voices from above recognize the youth in their midst, and as Gurnemanz had done before, they again proclaim, *"Enlightened by compassion the innocent fool wait for him, the appointed one!"*

Even though the voices remind the knights of the prophecy, they miss the point. They press Amfortas to serve, using the reminder manipulatively. It is sad that even though the knights regularly participate in their Love Feast, they fail to acquire compassion, and hence fail to become enlightened. Ironically, the bringer of redemption could have been any one of them; through compassion, any of the knights could have regained the *Will-to-Give* and restored Divine reality to the group. They could have returned the symbol of the Spear to its rightful place, and Amfortas would have been healed. But the religion established by Titurel and followed by the knights and squires shrouded Divine truth; they only saw dogma and symbols. Thus the Spear was lost and Divinity concealed.

Amfortas is again urged by Titurel to uncover the Grail. With great difficulty Amfortas rises. The squires remove the Grail from the shrine and its covering, and the voices proclaim:

VOICES
(from above)

Take this My blood, take this My body, in the name of our love.

(Amfortas reverently tends to the cup in silent prayers. Twilight spreads through the hall.)

BOYS
(from high up, where it's most dark)

Take this My blood, take this My body, in remembrance of Me.

(A blinding beam of light from above penetrates downward on the cup. They glow increasingly more and more in bright crimson. Amfortas with transfigured face, raises the Grail high and gently swings it toward all sides. Then he blesses the bread and wine. All are already fallen on their knees and raise their sight devoutly to the Holy Grail.)

TITUREL
Oh holy bliss! How brightly our Lord greets us today!

At this point in *Parsifal*, religion and the Divine meet in the same space, yet are worlds apart. The voice of the Divine, sung from above is heard, *"Take this My blood, Take this My body, in the name of our love. ...in remembrance of Me! ..."*. The first culmination of Wagner's message of this drama is displayed here. Though the Grail is revealed, its purpose is ignored and shrouded by the religiosity of Titurel and the knights. Only in the otherworldly voices of the youths, the truth and purpose of the Grail is revealed to us, the observers. While many may think the action of Amfortas serving the Holy Sacrament to the knights is wondrous, it is actually a negation of its true meaning. The Grail, or the *Will-to-Receive-from-the-Divine*, is present. It desires all to receive and be united with It. But rather than receive and be united, the father of the religion, Titurel, builder of all that conceals the Divine, misdirects the focus. It sounds so pious, so honest, so true, but it is like the serpent in the Garden that says:

"PARSIFAL: THE WILL AND REDEMPTION"

"For God knows that in the day you eat of it your eyes will be opened, and you will be like God, knowing good and evil."[53]

In the opening of the eyes to the Knowledge of Good and Evil, we actually shut our eyes to the Divine, the Tree of Life.[54] You cannot behold both at the same time. To uncover one is to cover the other. You either have dogma and symbology, or you have Divine reality. Titurel, the knights and sadly Amfortas, are victims of their own dogma and symbology. Worse yet, it is shrouded in and clouded by the beauty of religious practice.

Looking back, the angels never commanded Titurel to build a shrine for the relics to protect them from the world. Rather, they were given as a gift to humanity for healing and redemption. Yet, as Wagner's text reveals, Titurel did the opposite and built both castle and shrine. Those Divine realities needed no protection from humanity. They were potentially the sustenance that could give Life and Transformation to humanity. By enshrining Life, he in effect erected a *false spirit*; he was only protecting his possession. His own name should give us pause; *Titurel* is Aramaic meaning *Protector of God*. Why would God, the omniscient and omnipotent Creator of the universe, need protecting?

Valhalla was built to ensure Wotan's and the gods' safety, and to empower them to conquer foes who might threaten them and their possessions. As noted in the last chapter, Monsalvat is Valhalla resurrected. So too is Titurel the resurrected Wotan. In *Götterdämmerung* Act I, Scene 3, as Waltraute explains to Brünnhilde the state of affairs in the hall, Wotan sits on his throne silent and motionless. He only whispers his desire for Brünnhilde to return the Ring to the Rhinemaidens. He has stopped eating Holda's Apples; he is dying but not yet dead. In similar fashion, Titurel is silent and motionless. Like Wotan, he no longer can engage in battles or execute his office. He too is dying but not yet dead; the only thing keeping him alive is the decaying edifice of his old religion. If the Grail were to be revealed in its truest form and stripped of the religion that enshrines it, he would die - which is an indication of what is coming in Act III.

The voices are heard again from above, reaffirming what we heard before. The Body and Blood of Christ are *"... the loving spirit of blessed consolation ..."*. Parroting the same words, the knights join the voices, however with a subtle religious twist that once again shrouds Divine intent:

KNIGHTS
Take of the bread turn it confidently into bodily strength and power; true till death unwavering in effort, to work the Savior's will!

Take of the wine, convert it to the fiery blood of life. Joyous in the club, in brotherly faith to fight with holy courage!

Why *"Joyous in the club"* for the translation, rather than the more common, *"Joyous in unity ..."* ? In German the word *einheit* may have been a better choice if one was trying to communicate *oneness* or *unity*. However, *verein* is the word the knights use in the text; although it implies a sort of unity, it is more of an *association*, like being in a *club*. So again, we have the knights in a religious club, in contrast to being in true union with the Divine.

The final words of the knights are *"Blessed in faith! Blessed in love!"* Then the voices from above utter the same words. Ponder for a moment how they use the same words, yet their meanings are so different. One is about affiliation to beliefs, dogma, symbols and cause; while the other speaks of Divine Love, transformation and redemption.

As Amfortas is carried out on his bed, and all the knights and squires exit the hall, Gurnemanz and the youth remain. The youth was deeply affected by what happened,

"PARSIFAL: THE WILL AND REDEMPTION"

according to the stage directions. However, he seems bewildered; he keeps clutching his chest, shaking his head:

GURNEMANZ
Why are you standing there?

Do you know what you've seen?

(Parsifal presses his heart convulsively and shakes his head a little.)

So you are only a fool then!

(He opens a narrow side door.)

There! On your way! But listen to Gurnemanz: in the future leave the swans here in peace; a gander should search for a goose!

(He pushes Parsifal out and hits the door annoyingly upon him.)

The youth appears not to have been affected by the religious service as Gurnemanz had hoped. However, the youth was affected in ways Gurnemanz could not imagine. The suggestion is that Gurnemanz would have hoped the youth would have been enlightened by what he saw. Not, however, by compassion, but by cause. That he would have been moved by the Love Feast as proclaimed by the knights and realize that he had been called into the service of the Grail - that he would also finally realize the need of the knights and of Amfortas and leave on a holy quest to conquer Klingsor and return the Spear. But no! That is not what this youth heard or observed. Rather he heard a voice, *one that no one else heard;* and he saw a vision, *one that no one else saw.*

Before Gurnemanz expelled the youth, he said (as quoted above) *"... leave the swans here in peace; a gander should search for a goose!"* Again, we have the suggestion of Masculine and Feminine being united. However, rather than the symbolism of the swan, Gurnemanz calls the youth a gander. He did not realize to whom he was speaking. He did not perceive the spiritual potential within our youth; the swan of the higher world. To seek a goose would be to seek his feminine counterpart thoughtlessly. Then, as Gurnemanz follows where the knights exited, the voices from above can be heard a final time:

A VOICE
(from high up)

Enlightened through compassion, the innocent fool.

VOICES
(echoing from above)

Blessed in faith!

The prophecy has changed! No longer is it *"Enlightened through compassion, the innocent fool, wait for him ..."* - now it is *"Enlightened through compassion, the innocent fool ... blessed in faith"*. No longer is he waiting; he has arrived. No longer is he just an innocent fool, something has happened to him - deep in his heart something has touched him. He has been moved by and, as the voices proclaimed, blessed in something new ... *faith.*

The curtain falls.

ACT II

"EXPLORING RICHARD WAGNER'S FINAL TREATISE"

"PARSIFAL: THE WILL AND REDEMPTION"

Part I: The Obliviousness of Enlightenment

The curtain rises and we see a dark castle filled with magical and necromantic apparatus. Klingsor is off to one side against the wall gazing into a mirror. In the occult world there are several names for this practice, one of the most common of which is catoptromancy. Similarly to gazing into a crystal ball, it offers the ability to look into the past, present and future. It also offers the user the ability to peer into his deeper spiritual self. Hence, Klingsor and his castle are in a sense the mirror image of Titurel and Monsalvat; one the deeper self of the other. One is also the reflection of the other or, as when one looks in a mirror, the inverse of the other - so, the same, but inverted.

On the surface Klingsor is the antithesis of Titurel. Titurel is supposedly the noble knight who founded and established the Castle of the Grail in the name of all that is good. Although Titurel is noble externally, he is also empty and magical, like Klingsor. Klingsor is of a dark world; but so is Titurel. Because Titurel built the shrine and concealed the Divine relics, he too has in a sense used magic, even perhaps occultism. Inasmuch as Titurel's castle has all the pious trappings that exchange Divine reality for religion, in Klingsor's castle we see no Divinity - only manipulation of the natural world. How can they be the same? - one is good and the other is evil. In their own ways, both could be considered to be part of the Tree of the Knowledge of Good and Evil. Although they may appear to represent opposing forces, both are essentially egoistic (i.e., the Serpent; the *Will-to-Survive*, the *Will-to-Live*, the *Will-to-Receive-for-Itself-Alone*).

The curtain rises in the world of Enlightenment, the world of humanistic arrogance, in contrast to haughty religious bondage. Even with all the tools of the occult at his disposal, Klingsor doesn't use them as a child of the devil, but one who is superior, a man who has learned the physics and metaphysics of his world. He commands his realm with intellectual superiority. He manipulates Kundry through his ability to direct her psychologically and spiritually. There is no God in this domain, only the achievement of Man:

> KLINGSOR
> The time has come! My magic castle lures the fool, whom I see approaching from afar, shouting childishly. In deathly sleep the woman is held fast by the curse whose grip I have the power to loosen. Up then! To work!
>
> Come up! Come up! To me! Your master calls you, nameless one, she-devil, rose of hell! You were Herodias, and what else? Gundryggia there, Kundry here! Come here! Come hither, Kundry! Your master calls: obey!

He conjures Kundry from her sleep calling her several names, but he first calls her, *"... nameless one ..."*. Why is this soul, already named as Kundry, *nameless?* Because when this soul began its primordial journey, it too was nameless, like our youth. In the World of the Grail, to be nameless is to know one's true identity being in union with the Divine Source.[55] (We will explain this further later in this chapter.) In Klingsor's World of Enlightenment, knowing your name is not the same as in the World of the Grail. Knowing your name is to know your individual identity; thus the more you 'know', the more you are Enlightened, the more you grow. In contrast, the spiritual World of the Grail reveals through union with the Divine Source as your identity is found. Thus the more you are wedded to the Source, the more you are aware of who you are. In Kundry's case, she has been named and defined by the world around her, Klingsor's world and prior to that, Titurel's world. Even when she attempts to seek her 'wholeness', she can't find it because at best she is still *Kundry*.

Klingsor gives her two other names - *she-devil*, and *rose of hell*. Why those names? regarding her first name, *she-devil* in English lacks an important prefix that is present in the German. Klingsor calls her *Urteufelin*. The word *teufelin* by itself means *she-devil*, but Wagner added the prefix *Ur*, which means *from the very beginning*. A few librettos translate this as *primeval witch*. A better way to translate this would actually be *primeval she-devil*. But who is the primeval she-devil? In certain circles of the early Church, there was one who was given that name. One church writer had a vehemence toward women like no other. His name was Tertullian, born 160 AD. He is generally classified as an ecclesiastical writer, not as an early Church father. Despite this, he still became well known by Church leaders for the last two millennia for his horrendous views on women. In his book *The Apparel of Women* (Book 1, Introduction) Tertullian writes:

> *"And do you not know that you are (each) an Eve? The sentence of God on this sex of yours lives in this age: the guilt must of necessity live too. You are the devil's gateway: you are the unsealer of that (forbidden) tree: you are the first deserter of the divine law: you are she who persuaded him whom the devil was not valiant enough to attack. You destroyed so easily God's image, man."*[56]

As time passed Tertullian's influence faded but once out of the bag, his views never entirely disappeared - thus the *primeval she-devil* was Eve, herself.

Before we discuss the *rose of hell*, let's return to the proclamation, *nameless one*. For many of us who learned our Bible stories in Sunday School, God created a man called Adam, and from his rib He created a woman called Eve. But the text does not say that; Eve doesn't receive her name until *after* the Fall, in *Genesis 3:20*. Incidentally, the man also received his name, Adam, as an individual, after the Fall in *Genesis* 3:17. Prior to then, they were both called, Adam.

In Biblical Hebrew, names are functions, not mere labels of identity. In the Bible, people were not named because their relative had that name or because his or her parents liked that name. Rather, they were named because of the spiritual environment and occurrences that created the manifestation of their soul. So for example, the name, Jesus, the Greek rendering of the name Joshua, which in Hebrew is יְהוֹשׁוּעַ an imperfect tense verb meaning, 'Yah delivers'. Thus, Joshua was the deliverer of the people of Israel taking them into the Promised Land. In the same way, Jesus, יֵשׁוּעַ is 'Yah delivering' humanity from their sins.

Adam also is a *function* - the image and likeness of God. Adam had a masculine attribute and a feminine attribute. Because they were the image and likeness of God, they were *one being* with, in a sense two Divine attributes, a masculine *Will-to-Give*, and a feminine *Will-to-Receive-and-Give-Back-Again*.

Wagner's use of Klingsor's proclamation, *she-devil from the very beginning* has a twofold meaning. First, it is the identity that Kundry represents. Prior to the Fall the issue was not that Eve was nameless, but that her identity was one with Adam. They were a functionally one, the likeness of the Divine. At the Fall, at the Tree of the Knowledge of Good and Evil, that Divine union separated. After the Fall, Adam functioned as the image of the 'male' Serpent, and did something worse than Eve did; he blamed God for giving her to him, placing the responsibility of his failure on God. This is the first incidence of self-justification and Divine accusation:

> *"'Yes', Adam admitted, 'but it was the woman you gave me who brought me some, and I ate it.'"* **57**

This is the state of Klingsor's world - the world of the late Age of Enlightenment, and of the philosophical conflicts of Wagner and Nietzsche who believed that belief in God and religion contributes to our woes. Followers of the Enlightenment believed that reliance on religion indicated immaturity - that it was a prop to support emotional and intellectual frailty. It was thought that the 'enlightened' did not need such help; they could deal with reality by themselves, without religion, and could and would develop and grow to a higher state of being (only) through evolution. Today, in the 21st Century, proponents of these ideas (which were included in Nietzsche's worldview) include authors like Richard Dawkins and Lawrence Krauss. Nonetheless, those who argue that religion has much to do with war and suffering over the last two millennia would do well to remember that the Third Reich's 'Final Solution' wasn't authored by religionists, but by *'enlightened'* minds of the day.

Wagner wants to convey that the Enlightenment belief that (traditional) religion is a contributor to our woes and immaturity is in fact correct, but he also wants to tell us that 'the Divine' is denied by that same Enlightenment, which is as bad or worse than those woes and immaturity. At the very least, Enlightenment followers will say that there may be 'something' out there, but because they cannot perceive it, it does not exist for them. Thus, like the Serpent, we take pride in our questions, rather than in humility through our questions seeking answers. Almost prophetically, Wagner proclaimed that within the next 50 years this new approach to Enlightenment thought would promote barbarism.**58**

From this point on in Act II, in the 'lower world' of time, space and matter, the expression of the Divine is concealed because of the separation of Masculine and Feminine; it is only in their union that the Divine is revealed. Note that the author (and Wagner) are not referring here to male and female physical bodies, but to the spiritual qualities of Masculine and Feminine as defined in the Bible, Buddhism, Hinduism and Kabbalah.

Wagner's use of Klingsor, is in part to reveal the abuse of those in the Church, like those who supported Tertullian's view of women. Eve is not a *she-devil*, but actually a *redeemer*. Where Adam proclaims the woman's name after the Fall, there are often problems with most English versions of the Bible. The Hebrew phrase of *Genesis 3:20* is:

וַיִּקְרָא הָאָדָם שֵׁם אִשְׁתּוֹ **חַוָּה**
כִּי הִוא הָיְתָה אֵם כָּל־חָי:

The word *Chavah* (black, above) means, *Life-Giver*. Wagner was familiar with 'original' versions of the Old and New Testaments, and rarely read them in German. When Wagner read the Bible, and for that matter any of the Greek philosophers, he read them in Greek; Wagner read classical Greek fluently since the age of 12. So when Wagner was reading the Bible, he was less likely to be influenced by dogmatic, translated Catholic or Protestant nuance. Rather he read the text in a form closer to the original, and then developed his own point of view.

The Greek Old testament text that Wagner read was called the Septuagint, which is thought to have been the first translation to Greek from the original Hebrew, created in about the 3rd century before Christ. The *Genesis 3:20* text in Greek looks like this:

καὶ ἐκάλεσεν Αδαμ τὸ ὄνομα τῆς γυναικὸς αὐτοῦ **Ζωή**, ὅτι αὕτη μήτηρ πάντων τῶν ζώντων.

The word in the Septuagint used to translate *Chavah*, was *Zoe* (black, above), which is one of the most powerful, and frequently used words in the Bible. *Zoe (Ζωή)* is the correct

"PARSIFAL: THE WILL AND REDEMPTION"

translation for the woman's name in *Genesis 3:20*. Later in *Genesis 4:1*, the Greek text refers to her as *Eva (Ευαν)*, which means, to *proclaim, reveal* and *publish.* The reason for this is that *Chavah*, has a dual meaning. Not only is she the *Life-Giver*, but the *proclaimer* and *revealer* of that Life. The Biblical text is clear; the woman (Zoe/Eve) is a manifestation of redemption, as much as the Christ is the giver of it. Once again we have a union of Masculine and Feminine.

Another example of the union of Masculine and Feminine comes from the famous verse proclaiming salvation in the Gospel of John:

> *"For God so loved the world that He gave His only begotten Son, that whoever believes in Him should not perish but have everlasting life."*[59]

The phrase that describes eternal salvation here is, *everlasting life.* In Greek it is pronounced, *zoen aionion (ζωὴν αἰώνιον)*, which of course is the name of the woman we commonly call Eve in *Genesis.* 'Eve', or better said, 'Zoe', is *eternal Life!* The Feminine gave Life to Christ, the Redeemer, through the virgin birth. Christ in return gives that same Life, the Divine Feminine, the Cup (the Grail) to humanity. Thus, the *Will-to-Give*, is given. The *Will-to-Receive*, receives and gives back again. The union and circle of Eternal Life, the Tree of Life, perpetuates.

Wagner was not just aware of this, and was not just making small, honorable mention of it here. Actually, he places us intentionally here in the middle of a milieu of conflict and redemption. He makes sure that, like Senta, Elizabeth, and Brünnhilde before her, Kundry is a redeemer and giver of Life. However, here at the start of Act II, we are not yet supposed to be aware of this.

Having settled for the moment why Kundry is called first the *nameless one,* and the *primeval she-devil,* let's now discuss the name, *rose of hell.*

Beyond Schopenhauer and Nietzsche there is another German philosophy and theological practice that had been prevalent for almost 150 years by the time Wagner was penning *Parsifal*. It was supposed to be a secret society called the *Rose-Cross*, espousing *Rosicrucianism*. Some have erroneously associated Wagner with these concepts, but actually he was diametrically opposed to them.

In Bayreuth from 2008 to 2012 a wonderful production of *Parsifal*, presented by Stefan Herheim, addressed this notion. From the beginning, all the proper symbolisms were present. During the Prelude, a woman was seen writhing in a bed, set in the main room of Wagner's home in Bayreuth, Haus Wahnfried. It was as if she was giving birth and behind her projected on a huge curtain was a large red rose. The Herheim production was about how the misuse and misconnection of *Parsifal* with Rosicrucianism occurred swiftly after Wagner's death, and how that mentality and such secret societies affected Germany through the First World War. The culmination was in Act II, which was staged to take place during the Second World War. Klingsor's Garden, now the back yard of Haus Wahnfried, was adorned with large Nazi flags and a large stylized eagle with a Swastika in the middle. In both the first and second acts, whenever the Wahnfried garden is shown, Wagner's grave was placed where the prompter cover was located, at the front of the stage closest to the audience. Thus it was as if the audience was standing behind the grave watching what was happening. When Parsifal regained the spear from Klingsor, he plunged it into Wagner's grave to cleanse all the misnomers attributed to him and to his work. In Act III, rather than the events taking place at Wahnfried, they took place at the Bayreuth Festival Theater. Without giving away the ending, the true message of *Parsifal* was thus restored, and redemption was offered to the audience.

Rosicrucianism was supposedly founded by a man named Christian Rosenkreuz, in medieval Germany. While

"PARSIFAL: THE WILL AND REDEMPTION"

tradition has it that that was his name, actually that name was a play on words; 'Christian Rosenkreuz' translates to *Christian Rose Cross*. The key Rosicrucian symbol was a rose that appears, in different artistic depictions, upon the Cross of Christ. The Rosicrucians were part of the Freemasonry system. They believed that Jesus was not miraculously conceived, that he did not die on the cross, that his blood was never spilt and that he retired in the area of Mount Carmel after the years of his ministry. During the time of the Apostles there was a small sect that believed these ideas, long before Rosicrucianism was ever founded. They believed that Jesus deceived people into believing that he died on the cross, and later married Mary Magdalene and had a son. When Jesus then died of natural causes, Mary and her son set sail for the southern border of what is now called France, and raised their child, of Christ's royal blood. In the New Testament both the Apostle Paul and Apostle John addressed this belief system:

> *"Let no one deceive you by any means; for that Day will not come unless the falling away comes first, and the man of sin is revealed,* **the son of perdition,** *who opposes and exalts himself above all that is called God or that is worshiped, so that he sits as God in the temple of God, showing himself that he is God."*[60] *(bold emphasis added)*

> *"Dear children, the last hour is here. You have heard that the Antichrist is coming, and already* **many such antichrists have appeared.** *From this we know that the last hour has come. These people left our churches, but they never really belonged with us; otherwise they would have stayed with us. When they left, it proved that they did not belong with us."*[61] *(bold emphasis added)*

The son of perdition and the antichrists the Apostles spoke of were those that espoused this teaching. The ultimate antichrist for them was that so-called son of the blood lineage of Christ. This concept was rekindled on an international scale through Dan Brown's book, *The DiVinci Code*, which was based on several source materials, the main one being, *Holy Blood, Holy Grail* by Baigent, Leigh and Lincoln. Since the publishing of the book and others like it, portions of the historical findings have been debunked by independent authorities not related to the Church. But such deflations only fuel the fire, of why this had to be kept a secret, adding to the conspiracy and excitement.

Long before the conspiracy theories of *Holy Blood, Holy Grail*, there were those who were espousing these ideas against the early Church, long before the early organization of the Christian religion. There is historical documentation that validates not so much the claims of these theories, but that there were those who claimed it. We can thus trace these beliefs from the Rosicrucians back through the Merovingians.

At this point in our discussion, we now arrive at the name of, *the rose of hell*. *The rose of hell* is the woman who birthed the *son of perdition*; hence, the purported son of Jesus is the son of that *rose of hell*.

Wagner is doing something here in Act II, which is so vast that it begs a moment of real contemplation. In Act I he assaults the superficiality of religion. In the beginning of Act II, he now indicts not only the Age of Enlightenment, but the conspiracy-based secret societies that were prevalent in Germany in his day. One key reason for this is that some of those who were part of the Enlightenment were also part of those societies.

Keep in mind, Adolf Hitler joined the Thule Society as a corporal after WWI and become indoctrinated to this way of thinking, which would later fuel his skewed, manic views of Germany and, needless to say, of Wagner.

After referring to Kundry as the *rose of hell*, Klingsor calls her *Herodias*. Herodias was mother of the famous Salome, who danced before Herod. She danced what tradition

"PARSIFAL: THE WILL AND REDEMPTION"

tells us was *The Dance of the Seven Veils*. While it sounding poetic, without going into detail, this would be the equivalent to Herod and his friends going to a 'gentlemen's club'. In other words, it involved lewd, erotic dancing that aroused them sexually. Biblically, Herodias and Salome discussed, prior to the dance what would excite Herod and his friends and would result in them giving her whatsoever she requested.[62] Ultimately, she and her mother conspired to have John the Baptist's head on a silver platter - and they succeeded.

After being called the wicked Herodias, she is called Gundryggia, and then finally, Kundry. We discussed at length the connection of Gundryggia and Brünnhilde, but here's an early quote from Wagner regarding that connection, from August 1860:

> *"This strangely horrifying creature who, slave-like, serves the Knights of the Grail, with untiring eagerness, who carries out the most unheard-of tasks, and who lies in the corner waiting only until such time, as she is given some unusual and arduous task to perform - and who at times disappears completely, no one knows how or where? ... When Parsifal, the foolish lad, arrives in the land, she cannot avert her eyes from him: strange are the things that must go on inside her; she does not know it, but she clings to him. ... Only the manner of execution can say anything here! - But you can gain an idea of what I mean if you listen to the way that Brünnhilde listened to Wotan."*[63]

This is one of the places where we can associate Wotan with Klingsor. But as we progress in understanding Titurel and the Castle of the Grail, along with Klingsor and his dark castle; we must remember, we're in a land where *time becomes space*. In other words, Titurel and Klingsor may appear to be two different people, but actually they are the same. They are like the Tree in the Garden from which they metaphorically originate; the tree that bears fruit containing both good and evil. Yet, branch, trunk and root are the same. In modern terms you could say they exist in inverted parallel universes with Parsifal being the constant. Wagner communicates this concept well.

We must also remember that Wotan's spear has been split in half by Siegfried, as indicated in the stage direction:

> *(Siegfried with one blow strikes the Wanderer's spear in two: a flash of lightning darts from it towards the summit, where the flames, glowing dully before, now break out more and more brightly. The blow is accompanied by violent thunder that quickly dies away. The fragments of the spear fall at the Wanderer's feet. He quietly picks them up.)*
>
> *(Siegfried: Act III, Scene 2)*

The Spear has been split in two! Wagner has set the stage for the two, Klingsor and Titurel, to be the same. In similar fashion that Klingsor afflicted Amfortas with the wound that will not heal, so too Titurel afflicts Amfortas by vexing the same wound. You could say from one perspective that the wound will not heal because Titurel demands Amfortas to keep reopening it.

At the conclusion of the first act, the curtain closed concealing the Castle of the Grail; hence, we never left the domain where movement in time and space ceased. Such would be the case, even though you were enjoying the Bayreuth Festival and stepped out of the opera house for approximately an hour and ten minute intermission; enjoying a Bratwurst and a cool Maisels Weisse Hefeweizen.

Now in the beginning of the second act, the curtain rises in Klingsor's castle. Like their rulers, the castles are like the single Tree from which they bud. Klingsor's castle is the contrast, or inversion of the Castle of the Grail; it is what the 'shroud of religion' created in one respect, while now it reveals the underlying *Ego*, the Serpent, that feeds both religion, and denial of the Divine. In Act I we saw the indictment of both

"PARSIFAL: THE WILL AND REDEMPTION"

Christendom and Buddhism, and really, every traditional religion in between. Now we will see the indictment of ancient Germanic legend and contemporary humanistic Enlightenment.

In the first act we saw how traditional religion, to quote Wagner, *"cloaks a false spirit, making itself out to be pious and holy"*.[64] In this act, we find not only the cloak removed, but we see the discarding of all that is Divine. Klingsor is a sorcerer; he manipulates the spiritual and natural world. He is god in his own eyes, and there is no God other than himself. To possess the Grail would be to conquer all that has made itself out to be God, making himself supreme. Possessing the Grail presumes to be at the apex of the evolutionary diorama. To conquer the Grail would be to show that the only God that exists is 'evolving' man. This is the core of Rosicrucianism, the secret societies and the Enlightenment philosophy of Wagner's day. For Wagner at this moment, he is taking on virtually all perspectives of the Enlightenment in order to reveal his message. One might call this arrogance on Wagner's part, or the penetrating genius of a still flawed person seeking redemption who has found some measure in it and now has a message to proclaim.

There are two important points that need to be made at this juncture. Some have said that Wagner rejected Christianity and totally embraced Buddhism, claiming that at the time of his death he was working on yet another opera called *The Victors (Die Sieger)*. This is actually not true. Wagner throughout 1882 was reprinting all of his works as a testament of his life's journey; he wasn't doing that to proclaim his affirmation of the writings as present truths or works, but as a chronology of his life. Wagner himself said on July 10, 1882, just eight months before his death and at the beginning of the first Festival that would perform *Parsifal:*

"More than 25 years ago I sketched out a scenario on a single side of paper and gave it the

name: the Victors. Since conceiving Parsifal, I have altogether abandoned this Buddhist project - which is related to the former only in a weaker sense, - and since that time have given no further thought to elaborating on the sketch, still less of reading it aloud."[65]

Wagner was never against the truths of Christianity or Buddhism, but he was against the religiosity that masked the truths within them. Wagner took on the ancient legends and the Enlightenment, and seems to have had a prophetic view of the future. In that sense, he countered the views of the Catholic Church, as, for example, espoused by Constantin Franz. In *Federalism as the guiding principle for the social, governmental and international organization,* Frantz in 1879 supports the Catholic Church (specifically, in its form as the old Holy Roman Empire) as the solution to the woes of the German people. Frantz presents the Church as the extension of Christ, who is a man of peace, that should govern Germany:

"*If the Church [Roman Catholic] claimed to be the 'real organ of Christian ideas ... it must also be part of its function to encourage the people and their governments through teaching and admonition to work towards the possibilities of the foundation of an international organization'; by which he meant a federal Germany, and, eventually a federal Europe.*"[66]

Wagner, already having elaborated in earlier writings that religion with its dogmatic symbols destroyed the revelation of who Christ is, responds that, not only does he see that Rome has all but removed the reality of Christ from itself, he also knows full well of the rising Germanic cults like Rosicrucianism and the doctrines of Enlightenment, which are bringing to bear another type of nationalism. Wagner responds, July 14, 1879:

"*I am writing you immediately after finishing your 'Federalism' ... how similar to my own position I*

"PARSIFAL: THE WILL AND REDEMPTION"

find yours to be! ... And this brings me to the one aspect of your theory which causes me misgivings. You locate the realm of history in the sphere of man's 'free will', whereas I can see the freedom of the will only in the act of denying the world, i.e., in the advent of the "kingdom of grace". If the realm of history were to offer us anything other than the workings of an arbitrary despotism - which certainly does not mean freedom of the will, but rather the subjection of the will to blind self-interest ... I believe very definitely that this is the only outcome that now remains open to us; and historical analogies enable me to foresee our return to a state of barbarism around the middle of the next millennium. The man of peace whom you hold out to us presupposes too much reason on the part of the human race; unfortunately, moreover, there is no religion that can guide us along the right path, since - in my own estimation - this must first be revealed to us, and Jesus Christ must first be recognized and imitated by us." [67]

For Wagner, the Church, other religions, ancient occult societies and the Enlightenment are all progressing to the barbarism that he foresees. With all of this we cannot help but to acknowledge that Frantz's point of view, not to mention Wagner's in other writings, also created fertile ground for an anti-Semitic Germany of a new kind. The irony is that Wagner who would absolutely agree with such views, yet began backing away from what was rising in the German psyche. He wrote to Angelo Neumann in Berlin regarding the particular direction of the anti-Semitism in Germany on February 23, 1881:

"I have absolutely no connection with the present 'anti-Semitic' movement: an article of mine which is shortly to appear in the Bayreuther Blätter will prove this so conclusively that it will be impossible for

any of intelligence to associate me with that movement."[68]

The article was called *Know Thyself*, it was first published in 1881 in his *Religion and Art*[69]. We will discuss a bit more on this later.

As we return to Klingsor's castle, we must return to a state of mind where *time has become space.* Klingsor conjures Kundry. He mocks her service to the Grail knights, highlighting their lack of acceptance of her and that her deeds culminate in rejection. Her only desire is rest, a ceasing from her endless works to correct an uncorrectable wrong, regardless of her many lives.

KLINGSOR
Did another wake you? Huh?

KUNDRY
Yes ... my curse! O Yearning ... yearning!

The question is asked, *"Did another wake you?"* Klingsor elaborates by reiterating to Kundry, and for our benefit, that the one who woke her is yet another person she can right her wrong with.[70] But to do that she must confront him and be subject to the similar passion and scenario as before. Kundry refuses, but to no avail. Klingsor reminds her he has power over her because he will not (cannot) yield to her sexual wiles. Kundry mocks him in return.

KUNDRY
(laughing shrilly)

Ha ha! Are you chaste?

KLINGSOR
(furiously)

Why do you ask this, accursed witch?

(He sinks into gloomy brooding)

"PARSIFAL: THE WILL AND REDEMPTION"

Awful distress! So now the fiend mocks me that once I strove after holiness?

Awful distress! The pain of untamed desire, most horrible, hellish impulse which I had strangled to deathly silence - does it now laugh aloud and mock through you, bride of the devil?

Beware! One man already repents his contempt and scorn, that proud man, strong in holiness, who once drove me out. His race I ruined; unredeemed shall the guardian of the holy treasure languish; and soon - I know it - I myself will guard the Grail - Ha ha! How did you like the hero Amfortas whom I ensnared to your charms?

Klingsor's spite for Titurel is clear. But is this really about chastity? Titurel had a son, Amfortas, and we have no back story about his mother. If this were only about the having or not having of sex, we would miss the point here. This entire drama is about revealing the Divine, which comes through the union of the masculine and feminine spiritual qualities. That union in the world of time, space and matter we see as sex. But in the world where *time becomes space,* we are not speaking of the sexual act, but the uniting of the qualities of male and female. To properly unite these qualities, there has to be Divine Love; in other words, *Compassion.* This is about the *Will-to-Give* and the *Will-to-Receive* and the giving back of what was received again and again; creating the eternal cycle of limitless Life. But the *Will-to-Receive-for-Oneself-Alone,* the *Will-to-Survive,* the *Will-to-Live,* the *Will-to-Protect* one's possessions, only take for itself. Titurel is the *Will-to-Protect,* where Klingsor has become the *Will-to-Survive.* Amfortas is the *Will-to-Receive-for-Himself,* where the knights are the *Will-to-Live-for-Themselves.*

Kundry at this point is quite revealing. She's bound by something that keeps her from the inner rest she so desires.

It's a lie that Klingsor tells her, which plagues her and keeps her trapped in torment.

> KLINGSOR
> Ha! Who defies you will set you free, try with this boy who is coming.

This is similar to the experience Kundry has with the knights where she serves and is rejected for her service. But we are now in the dimension where there are no religious cloaks to mask what is really going on in the realm of desire. It's the Garden of Eden all over again! However, this isn't about the united image and likeness of God, about Adam and his/their Fall. This is about the potential of reuniting the masculine and feminine attributes either with selfish intention, lust; or Divine love and compassion. If it is the former, we have more of the same; if it is the latter, we have redemption. For Kundry she must lure her counterpart and then be rejected by him! Regardless of how you look at this, it is torturous. Being rejected is not what will free Kundry. Though as Act II progresses it will appear that that is what will happen. But it will not be her rejection that sets her free. There is only a partial truth there and from what we are just about to learn from Sir Ferris, one of Klingsor's knights, it is that partial truths lose their weapons quickly.

As the youth approaches Klingsor summons his knights. On the surface, we are told in the first act that these knights were those who fell to Klingsor's temptresses. But now we are in a land where time becomes space. Remember that Wagner told us in Act I, through Gurnemanz, when we entered the castle that the knights pledged themselves to the cause of the Grail. However, our knights in Act II under Klingsor's rule have no perception of the Divine, only to peer through the veil of their self-interest and desire for gratification with the flower maidens; whose underpinning motive is egoistic, or as Wagner wrote to Constantin Frantz, "... *blind self-interest* ...". Klingsor is the other side of the

"PARSIFAL: THE WILL AND REDEMPTION"

Titurel persona; his knights are no different. They are defending *their* Grail, the maidens of this realm. They intend to fight for their cause and to slay any foe that opposes them.

KLINGSOR
Ha! How they rush to the ramparts, my deluded garrison, to defend their beautiful witches! - Yes! Courage! Courage! - Ha ha! He is not afraid; he has disarmed brave Sir Ferris, whose weapon he sturdily wields against the throng.

Klingsor mentions one knight here, Sir Ferris, as Amfortas mentioned one knight, Gawain, in the first act. Sir Ferris in Wolfram von Eschenbach's *Parzival* is spelt Feirefiz. Sir Feirefiz was a Muslim and happened to be the half-brother of Parzival. It is amazing how Wagner doesn't leave any stone unturned. Sir Ferris is quickly vanquished by the youth, who at this point had no weapon. Remember in the first act, he broke his bow. What does this mean? The Muslim and Rosicrucian belief systems are congruent regarding the miraculous birth and the idea that Jesus never died on the Cross, but differ regarding virgin birth. Thus Feirefiz, or in *Parsifal*, Sir Ferris, is only the half-brother of Parsifal, because in effect he only has half of the truth. Thus he is vanquished quickly, despite Parsifal's lack of a weapon. The youth takes Sir Ferris' weapon and now triumphs over the rest of the knights who represent the contrary reality - they live under the spell that says there is no Divinity, no Christ's death, and thus no display of Divine compassion.

Once the youth moves beyond the battle, his attention is caught by Klingsor's beautiful Garden. The flower-maidens enter the garden using virtually the same words that the knights and squires did in the first act when the swan fell:

MAIDENS
Who is the scoundrel? Where is the scoundrel? Vengeance!

The maidens, as lovely as their music is, are not at all happy with the youth. As in Act I, when the youth arrived striking the swan, the knights and squires called him a scoundrel and wanted vengeance. Here too upon his arrival, he is called a scoundrel and vengeance is demanded, this time by the flower-maidens. Yet as soon as he acknowledges them, their attention instantly changes from their felled lovers to wanting the youth for sensual play. As they attempt interaction, they begin to fight over him. Remember our youth hasn't yet been tainted with the Knowledge of Good and Evil. Because of his ignorance of the Tree, he is still in a place of *choice.* He can choose the Tree of the Knowledge of Good and Evil *or* the Tree of Life.

"PARSIFAL: THE WILL AND REDEMPTION"

PART 2: THE CONFLICT OF REASON AND DIVINE REALITY

Our heroic youth wrests himself from the maidens and starts away from the garden. In that moment Kundry appears and calls him by name:

KUNDRY
Parsifal! Stay!

He pauses; and in a flash the name of our youth is revealed, Parsifal. When Wagner started working on this Sacred Stage Drama, the name of our hero went through a transformation. Regarding settling on the name Parsifal, Wagner said on November 22, 1877:

"This is an Arabian name. The old troubadours no longer understood what it meant. 'Parsi fal' means: 'parsi' think of the fire loving Parsees[71] 'pure'. 'fal' means 'mad' in a higher sense, in other words a man without sophistication, but one of a genius fellow', in English, seems to be related to this Oriental root." [72]

Hence, the name 'Parsifal' means 'pure madness', but also 'genius'; so by extension 'pure fool', which implies that he potentially has access to true intelligence:

PARSIFAL
Parsifal ...? Once dreaming my mother called me that.

Kundry's presence disperses the flower-maidens. As they leave, like Gurnemanz, with disdain they call him a fool. Disappearing from the garden, Kundry is revealed as a young woman, completely transformed, upon a couch of flowers. Parsifal then says something profound:

PARSIFAL
Did you call me nameless one?

To Parsifal, *she* is the *nameless one*. This has tremendous potential from the outset. We are in a type of Garden of Eden once again. However, this is not about the creature called Adam, with masculine and feminine attributes revealing the Divine. This is a garden where the two attributes enter separated, thus concealing the Divine, but with the opportunity to become one once again. But what has kept them apart?

As we noted earlier from Biblical text, prior to partaking of the Tree of the Knowledge of Good and Evil, the man and woman were both called, Adam. It wasn't that Eve didn't have a name, they were both the same:

> *"Male and female created he them; and blessed them, and called their name Adam, in the day when they were created."*[73]

However, there was a brief state where the Feminine was *nameless,* which was at the moment of the Fall and prior to the man naming her, *Zoe*. Keep in mind, the name she receives is *Life-Giver,* or *Eternal Life*.

Here we find our *nameless* youth being introduced to *his* name. This is why the author has referred to him as *"the/our youth"* until this moment, to suggest and emphasize the impact of who he was and what he has now just become.

Kundry calls *him* by name, yet he refers to her as *nameless one*. This is the reverse of what Christ did in the garden with Mary Magdalene after His resurrection, in the Gospel of John. There she saw Him as a nameless gardener.

"PARSIFAL: THE WILL AND REDEMPTION"

But when he called her by name, Mary, her eyes were opened, and she knew it was Jesus. By Kundry calling the nameless youth by his name, he is on the verge to become *knowing of* divinity - and it will not be of the Tree of the Knowledge of Good and Evil - it will be of the Tree of Life. This *knowing* is very contrary to Enlightenment 'knowing'. However, for Wagner, in his display of Divine reality, that is what true enlightenment is.

To be *nameless* is to be a reflection of the Divine. In other words, it is not one's individuality that can be seen by others, it is the Divine expressing *Itself* through that one. Taking on a name - Adam, Parsifal, Jesus - is in a sense fulfillment of a Divine purpose. Thus, to be *nameless* is to be in a Divine/Holy state. Kundry in her original state as the Divine Feminine would thus be *nameless*. Parsifal has addressed her true origin *(nameless)*, while she calls him based on fulfillment of Divine purpose (by virtue of his special name, Parsifal). We can now see the end taking shape; eventually, the two will be made one, and will no longer be only Parsifal or Kundry, but both again *nameless*, revealing the Divine.

Parsifal recalls that his name was once whispered by his mother while dreaming. In a world where time becomes space, where distance and time are no longer governed by the affairs of physical reality; awareness is a continuum not limited to past, present and future. It is more than a knowing, like when one is connected to the Tree of the Knowledge of Good and Evil, which by definition is Spiritual Death. *("But of the Tree of the Knowledge of Good and Evil you shall not eat, for in the day you eat of it you shall surely die."*[74]*)* It is a flowing awareness interconnected by all aspects of the Divine Source's spiritual quality, filled with the eternal creative force of the Tree of Life. To put this another way, this eternal creative force is revealed when all the feminine and masculine qualities are connected. This is what we are facing in Klingsor's Garden. From the flower-maidens, to Kundry, to

Herzeleide, and the Grail - all are connected in some way. In similar fashion, the knights, Titurel, Amfortas, Klingsor and Parsifal also are interconnected, but the Masculine and Feminine in them is not. There is no apparent bond in the 'lower world' of flesh and matter. Nevertheless, for the Divine to be revealed in the world of the five senses, it must first be revealed in the 'real' world where there is no time or distance. Wagner stated earlier that we are *co-creators with God at every moment*.

What does this mean? This is about creation, and in particular, God creating a creature of equal status and quality and yet doing so by *free will*. This brings us back to *Die Walküre*, Act II, Scene 1, when Wotan tells Fricka that he is trying to create a hero who, freed from Divine protection and thus freed from Divine law, would do what a god is prevented from doing. There are several layers to this statement. *At a primary level, a god that rules by laws is thus bound by the laws by which he rules.* This is the dilemma of the god's of the ancient world of the Nibelungen. The only way Wotan gained his power was through the laws and covenants that ratified those laws. When Siegfried broke Wotan's spear, that didn't void the contracts; rather it passed those contracts on to the new ruler, Siegfried. Therefore, Brünnhilde tells us at the immolation that Siegfried was caused to bear the curse that was to be upon Wotan. It is the principle that issues forth from the Knowledge of Good and Evil, which is consistent throughout *The Ring*. If you conquered a foe, you got both his treasure and his curse.

Keep in mind, that for Wotan this came about by giving up Freia (Holda) as payment for Valhalla. Wotan gave up that aspect that represented the Divine Feminine (his Eternal Life, and that of the other gods) to build a castle that would protect him, his family, and his possessions. In protecting what we possess, we give up the counterpart of ourselves and Divinity is lost from us. In other words, when we become the *Will-to-*

"PARSIFAL: THE WILL AND REDEMPTION"

Receive-for-Itself, we interrupt the cycle of Eternal Life *(Zoe)* and enslave it to separation from Divine intention.

In *The Ring*, when Freia was given to the Giants, the gods began to age and become mortal. Wotan's curse was not only in stealing the ring from Alberich, but also in being like Alberich, in his intentions. In the beginning of *Das Rheingold* Alberich gave up love, choosing power and dominion to gain that for which he lusted; thus, he transformed the gold into the infamous ring. Alberich is no different from Klingsor in that moment; he took that which is 'of nature' (gold), and enslaved it for his purposes, fashioning it into the coveted ring. In similar fashion, Wotan took that which is 'of nature' (fire, Loge), and enslaved it/him for his bidding. At the end of *The Ring*, all that Wotan tried to protect and enslave hastened his demise. After all, it is Loge/fire, as Brünnhilde commands at the end of *Götterdämmerung*, the very force 'of nature' that Wotan enslaved, that consumes Valhalla. In addition, Wotan, too gave up love for the lust of power and dominion. He gave up, Fricka, Freia, and even his own daughter Brünnhilde. His resolve was finally the *Will-to-Die*, or the *Will-to-Give-Up-This-World*. This was the first positive inclination in *The Ring*; the second was from Brünnhilde in her immolation. With this in mind, consider now where we are in *Parsifal*.

Kundry tells Parsifal that she was waiting for him to give him his name. She explains that it was the wish of his father, Gamuret, before he was born. Then she adds:

KUNDRY
I waited for you here to tell you this: what drew you here, if not the desire to know?

PARSIFAL
I never saw, nor dreamt, of what I now see, and which fills me with horror ...

Parsifal is pure and innocent, not of making mistakes, but of the Tree of the Knowledge of Good and Evil. He never dreamt of what Kundry is insinuating that he should 'know'. To contrast what is happening even more dynamically, we could say that the Tree of the Knowledge of Good and Evil, is in a sense a Tree of Death; the opposite to that which gives Life. Life is union with the Divine. Death, which has little to do with physical death, is the concealment or loss of that which is Divine. To be 'knowing' in the way Kundry knows, is Death - the concealment of that which is Divine. To conceal the Divine is to give the illusion that God does not exist.

Kundry immediately starts the process of awakening Parsifal's desire for knowledge. She tells him of a child upon his mother's breast. She identifies his mother by name, Herzeleide. She indicates to Parsifal that he was his mother's delight in the midst of sorrow after the loss of his father. Please note again, that we have in this scenario the separation of Masculine and Feminine; this time from the perspective of Herzeleide. Her husband, her male counterpart (in the union of marriage) was dead:

KUNDRY
She was managing the pain, child of sorrow, for your father's love and death. To protect you from like peril she deemed it her highest duty. She strove to hide and shelter you safe afar from weapons and men's strife and passion.

Once again we repeat the same, echoing Wagner:

"... so if Man made a law to shackle love, to reach a goal that lies outside of human nature (namely, power, dominion - above all: the protection of property), he sinned against the law of his own existence, and therewith slew himself".

Herzeleide too was in a state of Spiritual Death; she was protecting Parsifal from becoming a knight like his father. In protecting him, Herzeleide sinned against her own existence and thereby slew herself; the Divine is again concealed. Notice the cycle. Gamuret is slain; the Divine

"PARSIFAL: THE WILL AND REDEMPTION"

Masculine and Feminine is/are separated. In the state of separation, the Feminine tries to preserve what remnant she has of that which was once Divine. Yet, in protecting it, as Titurel does, she ultimately conceals it and loses what reality of the remnant she had.

Kundry tells Parsifal that his mother lost him to his roaming, but joyously found him again, though briefly. She reprimands him telling him he was inconsiderate of her and made matters worse by leaving her again - this time not to return, leaving no trace as to where he went. The tremendous pain of losing him caused her heart to break, and she died.

Success! Kundry gets the reaction she was hoping for. Like Gurnemanz, who in Act I placed guilt and shame, a fruit of the Tree of Death, upon Parsifal, so Kundry now does again. This time Parsifal takes on that blame. He weeps, calling himself a blundering fool. Now comes the extension of the Tree of Death, the offering of the Knowing of Good and Evil. She offers him the *"... solace which love offers you".* She suggests that she comfort his distress with her sensual love. However, Parsifal is oblivious to what Kundry is attempting. He is still overwhelmed with the grief and the loss of his mother:

KUNDRY
Confession will end guilt in remorse, understanding changes folly into sense. Learn to know the love that enfolded Gamuret when the passion of Heart's Sorrow engulfed him in its fire! She who once gave you life and being, to subdue death and folly sends you this day, as a last token of a mother's blessing, the first kiss of love.

(She has bent her head completely over his and gives him a long kiss on the lips.)

PARSIFAL
(Suddenly starts up with a gesture of the utmost horror: his countenance expresses some fearful

change; he presses his hands firm against his heart as if to master an excruciating pain.)

This is the fulcrum, transitioning all that has come before, to all that will follow. Thus far we have mentioned and discussed the Tree of the Knowledge of Good and Evil and its meaning, but here it all comes together. Many have speculated about what Kundry's kiss means, but the greatest authority to whom we can turn, is the master himself. Wagner explains to us on September 7, 1865 the meaning of Kundry's kiss:

> *"You know of course, the servants of Paradise and its tempting promise: 'Ye shall be as gods, knowing good and evil'. Adam and Eve became 'knowing'. They became 'conscious of sin'. The human race had to atone for that consciousness by suffering shame and misery until redeemed by Christ who took upon himself the sins of mankind. My dearest friend, how can I speak of such profound matters except in simile, by means of a comparison? But only the clairvoyant can say what its inner meaning may be. Adam plus Eve equals Christ. How would it be if we were now to add to them: Amfortas plus Kundry equals Parsifal? But with considerable caution. The kiss which causes Amfortas the fall into sin awakens in Parsifal a full awareness of that sin, not as his own sin, but as that of the grievously afflicted Amfortas whose lamentations he had previously heard only dully, but the case of which now dawns upon him in all its brightness, through his sharing the feeling of sin: with the speed of lightning he said to himself, as it were: 'ah! That is the poison that causes him to sink in whose grief I did not understand until now!' Thus he knew more than all the others, more especially than the assembled knights of the Grail who continued to think that Amfortas was complaining of merely a spear-wound! Parsifal now sees deeper. ... he who would*

"PARSIFAL: THE WILL AND REDEMPTION"

know of it must hear in my works themselves with ears with which superficial listeners cannot hear. Happily, it is an awareness not of sin but solely of redemption from the sin of the world. But who has divined this redemption in my works?"[75]

Parsifal in this moment has a choice, just like the man and woman had a choice before the Tree of the Knowledge of Good and Evil. As for the man and woman, they chose to eat of the tree; leading to Spiritual Death, and to concealment of the Divine. The Serpent promised, if you eat of this tree you will be like God. The deception of this statement was in the suggestion that they were not already like God; the man and woman were already the image and likeness of God. Partaking of that Tree implied doubt and denial of who they really were. The second aspect of the deception was that by partaking of the Tree, they would *know* good and evil, and thusly would attain *godlikeness*.

Wagner explains the relationship of this garden encounter by using an expression of logical inference:

if: Adam + Eve = Christ,
then: Amfortas + Kundry = Parsifal.

He unpacks this idea further by saying that when Adam and Eve partook of the Tree of the Knowledge of Good and Evil, they became 'knowing', they became *conscious of sin*. What was the sin? The false belief, or to use Wagner's words from earlier, embracing the *false spirit*, which includes the grandest of all deceits, that you and I are not the Likeness of God and we need to possess, in particular, the 'knowing' of good and evil to obtain it. Based on this primary fallacy, another and worse development occurs - the separation of Masculine and Feminine, the *Will-to-Give* and the *Will-to-Receive-and-Give-Back-Again*, leading to concealment of God, the Divine reality, and subsequently the Divine Image and Likeness. In its concealment, the illusion of a non-existent God becomes reality. This then becomes another *knowledge* to humanity, the 'knowing' that God doesn't exist. In this state, *"The human race had to atone for that consciousness by suffering shame and misery until redeemed by Christ who took upon himself the sins of mankind"*. We may believe that we are not like God and must learn good and evil to attain godliness, or we may believe that God does not exist and therefore we become our own god. In either case, Christian theology holds that Christ had to bear that/those sins - thus on the Cross He became both the unworthy and the unbelieving.

Now Wagner tells us that only the clairvoyant, the mystic, the spiritually intuitive will understand his meaning, *"The kiss which causes Amfortas the fall into sin awakens in Parsifal a full awareness of that sin, not as his own sin, but as that of the grievously afflicted Amfortas ..."*. In this moment, Parsifal also becomes 'knowing', not of the Tree of the Knowledge of Good and Evil (the Tree of Death), but of the Tree of Life. What Kundry awakens in Parsifal is Divine Compassion!

When Wagner speaks of Christ bearing the sin of humanity, he is speaking directly of a theological doctrine called, Identification and Substitution. Biblical teaching holds that Christ becomes us on the Cross and dies our death, a sinner's death. In other words, he becomes our substitute and identifies Himself as us. In the Resurrection, that identification still applies - he is raised as us, completely Divine, the resurrected Adam. In this identification we again embrace Divinity without the concern of knowing good and evil. We are because we are, not because of what we do. However, truly discovering who we are affects what we do. We embrace Divinity by denying the ego's desire (the Serpents nature) to be like God through the acquiring of knowledge and the doing of good and the shunning of evil. Rather, we accept the reality that we are Divine and through the ongoing discovery of that indwelling reality, we once again put on the image and likeness we always were intended to have.

"PARSIFAL: THE WILL AND REDEMPTION"

Another dynamic of this is what reveals Christ as Christ - Divine Compassion. As we mentioned before, Wagner said, *"... God will have revealed Himself with the entry of the most unshakeable truth into every domain of existence: the way from man to Him is compassion ..."*. If the religious embraced the doing of good and evil to be like God, which conceals Divine Reality; then what of those that claim there is no God? Wagner insists that the unbeliever, the so-called *Enlightened*, are faced with a display of compassion that can be regarded as Divine; or their compassion has to be disregarded because Enlightenment's egoism is too self-absorbed to consider such a reality. Nietzsche described this as weakness and defective, in, *Human, All-Too-Human*:

"The founder of Christianity, as is self-evident, was not without the greatest defects and prejudices ..."

Wagner said:

"It was otherwise with the Christian religion. Its founder was not wise, but divine; his teaching was the deed of free-Will suffering. To believe in Him, meant to emulate Him; to hope for redemption, to strive for union with Him."[76]

Parsifal clutches his chest! In so doing he addressed two very specific things. First, he proclaims:

PARSIFAL
Amfortas! - The wound! The wound! It burns within my heart! O sorrow, sorrow! Fearful sorrow! From the depths of my heart it cries aloud. Oh! Oh! Most wretched! Most pitiable! I saw the wound bleeding: now it bleeds in me!

Parsifal, like Christ, identified with Amfortas' suffering. He was not just aware of Amfortas' suffering, he felt it and perceived it as if it were his own. The wonder of this moment is that Parsifal chose not to partake of the Tree of the Knowledge of Good and Evil, which would have resulted in him judging Amfortas as a sinner. Rather through his inner sense he identified himself with Amfortas. But his identification with Amfortas' suffering was not the conclusion - it was only a gateway to his real, deeper suffering at the end Act I, at which time he did not fully understand it.

The second aspect of clutching his heart, is the experience of 'heart's sorrow', after all he said, *"... my heart! O sorrow ..."*. Not only does he experience Amfortas' suffering, he also becomes acquainted with the condition of Herzeleide. He now can identify with the feminine suffering of losing the masculine counterpart. In this moment there is an embryonic union of the Masculine and Feminine and the emergence of true Divinity. Within Parsifal, the two are becoming one:

PARSIFAL
(As Kundry stares at Parsifal in fear and astonishment, he falls into a complete trance.)

(in a low voice, with horror)

My dull gaze is fixed on the sacred vessel; the holy blood flows: - the bliss of redemption, divinely mild, trembles within every soul around: only here, in my heart, will the pangs not be stilled. The Savior's lament I hear there, the lament, ah! the lamentation from His profaned sanctuary: 'Redeem Me, rescue Me from hands defiled by sin!' Thus rang the divine lament in terrible clarity in my soul. And I - fool, coward, fled hither to wild childish deeds!

(He hurls himself in despair on his knees)

Redeemer! Savior! Lord of grace! How can I, a sinner, purge my guilt?

Parsifal heard what no one before him could. His identification with Amfortas' and his identification with Herzeleide's pain and loss, causes a joining of the masculine and feminine qualities of the Divine within himself. Within this embryonic union, the Savior is revealed to him, and he can

"PARSIFAL: THE WILL AND REDEMPTION"

recall the Savior Himself calling from the Grail, *"The Savior's lament I hear there ... ah! the lamentation from His profaned sanctuary: 'Redeem Me, rescue Me from hands defiled by sin!'"* The voice of the Savior within the Grail is crying out, *redeem me from the hands defiled by sin*. What is the sin? Was it Amfortas' behavior with Kundry that brought about the wound? Or is it the obscuring shrine that keeps the reality of the Divine concealed from its proper revelation and its proper home? It is the latter!

Titurel was the initial sinner who brought about the chain of events with which we are now contending. By creating the castle to protect what he was given, he shackled the Grail, the Cup that harbored Christ's blood - which is the revelation of Divine Compassion.

This is the key point of Wagner's *Religion and Art*, from which we quoted earlier. Wagner is now in the process of removing the symbols and dogmas of both religion and the reasoning of Enlightenment, to reveal Divinity. He is using Art to do what Religion could not. The Grail's cry is to be freed from the Domain of Religion and as we shall soon see, the Domain of Enlightenment. To put it another way, the Grail needs to be liberated from the false sanctuary in which it has been held as a protected possession. It needs to be returned to its rightful, Life-Giving sanctuary.

Kundry, as if the voice of 'reason' (Enlightenment) breaks through, tells Parsifal to *flee the delusion* and take her embrace! Yet, while still on his knees and as if seeing a vision, he realizes she was the one who wounded Amfortas.

PARSIFAL
(He has gradually risen to his feet.)

Ah! This kiss!

(He pushes Kundry away from him.)

Corrupter! Get away from me! Forever! Forever - keep away!

Parsifal had just previously cried out to Christ, *"Redeemer! Savior! Lord of grace! How can I, a sinner, purge my guilt?"* Parsifal's rejection of Kundry is not what has saved her at this point. Rather it is what has, in effect saved him. His compassion for those hurting, and in particular realizing the Saviors lament has put him in a position to resist the potential of his own lust, or *brute nature* and fall prey to what his predecessors did. Klingsor spoke earlier of Kundry being rejected for her salvation. Yet that salvation was not merely in her being rejected - it was really for the one who was rejecting. In Parsifal by sensing Egoistic, *Self-Will* lust, he became knowing, not of the Tree of the Knowledge of Good and Evil, but of the Tree of Life and Compassion. In his resistance, roused by compassion, he discovered Divinity. We will then see in the next Act that by *his* attaining compassion, Kundry will also attain it - the two will become one:

> KUNDRY
> Cruel one! If you feel in your heart only the sorrows of others, then feel mine as well! If you are a redeemer, what maliciously stops you from uniting with me for my salvation?

In one respect Kundry is correct, for her salvation to occur she must be united with her masculine counterpart. But united for selfish, egocentric, lustful reasons, only perpetuates more of the same - separation and concealment. She approaches Parsifal again with the intention to unite with him for lustful pleasure, *Self-Will*. As she approaches, she stops transfixed, recalling why she is shackled to her curse - *her* wound that will not heal.

Klingsor mentioned earlier that he had power over her because he would not fall prey to her feminine wiles. This is actually not fully true. Klingsor had power, yes, but because Kundry rejected the existence of God, and thereby rejected Divinity within herself. Thus, she was a slave to the base, the fallen, or as Wagner pens it, her *brute nature*.

"PARSIFAL: THE WILL AND REDEMPTION"

Kundry is controlled by her *brute nature*. She cannot suppress her egoism, her desire for self-gratification, because there is no discovered higher reality within her to permit that. In Enlightenment philosophy it is believed that there is no God; thus we are eventually, our own god. Man individually and collectively is the highest manifestation of the dogma of evolution. The 'human' in his own development within the confines of this world, as in Nietzsche's *Zarathustra*, attains the state of Übermensch *(Beyond-Human, or Superman)*. There is no eternal soul or spiritual world as in Christianity or Buddhism. Nietzsche penned in the *Also Sprach Zarathustra* Prologue:

> *"I love those who do not first seek beyond the stars for reasons to go down and to be sacrifices: but who sacrifice themselves to the earth that the earth may one day belong to the Superman."*[77]

The Superman aspect to Enlightenment philosophy was the ultimate attainment of the development of Man: Man helping himself to attain a kind of godhood. In contrast, the spiritual practices of the mystic are scoffed at. What is most interesting about this growing philosophy in the time of Wagner, and in the following half century is that it bears responsibility for the looming barbarism. By the time the Third Reich was in power, the same, original production of *Parsifal* had been being performed at Bayreuth for over 51 years.

However, not long after the death of Wagner's son Siegfried, his wife Winifred took the reign as director of the Festival. No sooner was she in charge, she disbanded the *Parsifal* production saying it needed *to take on the present-day Zeitgeist (the spirit of the time)* - so the production changed, radically. Many were horrified; it was called a 'desecration' and a 'sacrilege'. This rather strong reaction to the new production had nothing to do with any anti-Semitic, or German National points of view; these overtones were largely or completely absent in the original production.

In reaction to this news, over a thousand signatures were collected and published in *Figaro* (Paris) opposing the new production. At the top of this list demanding that the original production *("... upon which the eye of the Master had rested")* be preserved were Eva and Daniella Wagner, Cosima's daughters, Richard Strauss, and Arturo Toscanini. However, these production issues soon became moot because, just before the start of WWII the Reich Board of Arts and Culture, under the authority of Hitler directed that *Parsifal* would no longer be performed. Their reasoning was that the message of suffering and compassion were not appropriate in wartime.[78]

Hitler never really understood Wagner. Rather he saw what he wanted to see and created a Wagner for his own use, Hitler said:

> *"'I could find no cause for admiration', he recounted later, 'for the piddling Knights who dishonored their Aryan Blood to follow the superstitions of the Jew, Jesus. My sympathy was entirely with Klingsor'"*[79]

Clearly that was not Wagner's message. However, in light of what was about to be experienced between Kundry and Parsifal, Wagner was tackling both the attitude of the Enlightenment and, in particular the attitude of Nietzsche. Nietzsche wrote in *The Antichrist*:

> *"The Jews are the strangest people in world history because, confronted with the question whether to be or not to be, they chose, with a perfectly uncanny deliberateness, to be at any price: this price was the radical falsification of all nature, all naturalness, all reality of the whole inner world as well as the outer. ... That is precisely why the Jews are the most catastrophic people of world history: by their*

"PARSIFAL: THE WILL AND REDEMPTION"

aftereffect they have made mankind so thoroughly false that even today the Christian can feel anti-Jewish without realizing that he himself is the ultimate Jewish consequence. ... With this I am at the end and I pronounce my judgment. I condemn Christianity. ... Let anyone dare to speak to me of its 'humanitarian' blessings! To abolish its distress ran counter to its deepest advantages ... I call Christianity the one great curse, the great innermost corruption, the one great instinct of revenge ... I call it the one immortal blemish on mankind."[80]

Hitler would soon proclaim, *"The Superman is living among us now! He is here!"*[81]

In this moment of our Sacred Stage Drama, Wagner opens to us Kundry's powerless dilemma. She, like Nietzsche, the Enlightenment, the Rosicrucian and those who were of that mind dating back to the time of Christ, mocked the crucifixion:

KUNDRY

Oh! If you knew the curse which afflicts me, asleep and awake, in death and life, pain and laughter, newly fortified to new affliction, endlessly through this existence!

I saw Him - Him - and mocked...! His gaze fell upon me!

Now I seek Him from world to world to meet Him once again. In darkest hour I feel His eyes turn on me and His gaze rests upon me. Then accursed laughter assails me once again: a sinner sinks into my arms! Then I laugh - laugh!

The mockery of Christ is her curse. In her mockery she reveals her base nature, her *brute nature*. This is not just a denial of the purpose and existence of Christ, it is the mockery of it. Yet, deep within her, she seeks for His gaze again, hoping to conjure within herself a different response. In the Realm of the Grail she works for her salvation, as we shall see, to no avail. Religiosity alone cannot provide what the soul requires, and most definitely the mockery of Christ or religion only fuels the brute, egoistic nature within:

> KUNDRY
> One for whom I yearned in deathly longing, whom I recognized though despised and rejected, let me weep upon his breast, for one hour only be united to you and, though God and the world disown me, in you be cleansed of sin and redeemed!

Kundry recognized that she once despised and rejected the One for Whom she now longed. What a paradox! She desires the Divine, yet mocks its existence. Though blind to it, the Enlightenment resulted in selfish desire - the *Will-to-Receive-for-Itself*, the *Will-to-Survive.* We cannot attain Divinity by denying its existence. Enlightenment philosophy proclaimed that attaining human perfection (another way of saying godhood), or achieving Superman status, was possible without religion. However, attaining Divine status (perfection) through Enlightenment philosophy is not possible because that philosophy mocks the pathway by which Divine status will be attained. Wagner called this, *blind self-interest* and as we will discuss in Part 3, *a negation.*

Parsifal responds with a 'knowing' that suggests he is no longer (just) a simple fool. Rather, he now has insight and wisdom:

> PARSIFAL
> For your salvation too I am sent, if you will avert from your desires. The solace to end your sorrows comes not from the source from which they flow: grace shall never be bestowed on you until that source is sealed to you.

This is possibly the most profound statement within the entire opera. Kundry, who exists in the Dimension of the Grail,

"PARSIFAL: THE WILL AND REDEMPTION"

and in the dimension of Klingsor, faces two major challenges. In the world of Klingsor she mocked Christ, though she desired redemption, wholeness, and attaining an image and likeness of the Divine. In the World of the Grail, she worked (literally, doing good deeds) for her affirmation, acceptance, and salvation. However, her motivation in both cases was the sense of separation from the Divine and consequently her true identity. Regardless of whether she mocks or works, there is still the sense of separation; her false sense of separation creates the illusion that there is a need to work to attain the Divine, or the illusion of its non-existence.

Her second major challenge was her deep inner awareness of, and desire to be united with her masculine counterpart. However, in her wounded state, the *Will-to-Receive-for-Itself*, her only notion of union is in a brute, or base sense. Rather than recognize a possible Divine union, she perceives only a sensual one. This is not about sex, although on the surface it may seem that way; this is about *Ego, Self-Will*. Thus Parsifal profoundly tells her, *"The solace to end your sorrows comes not from the source from which they flow ..."*. The depth and profound dynamics here can take many years to truly embrace. Parsifal is telling Kundry that her 'source' must change; that she will *not* find consolation from the same source that is causing her distress. Hence, religion cannot bring true consolation through religion alone, and Enlightenment cannot bring consolation through its reasoning alone - Wagner would hold that both of these pathways are self-deceiving illusion.

Expounding on Parsifal's statement in the Wagnerian context of time becoming space, Kundry was trying to comfort her woes from the *Will-to-Receive-For-Itself*, the *Will-to-Survive*, the *Ego*. However, her *Ego* was causing the very woe she was trying to console. Self-medication by drug and alcohol abuse is an obvious example of this kind of thinking, but this concept also applies to our religions and philosophies. In Wagner's case, he was applying this in very broad, focused strokes to the evolutionary development of Man; he was addressing religion which claims to house God, and the Enlightenment which claims there is no God:

PARSIFAL
... salvation shall never be bestowed on you until that source is sealed to you. Another - ah, a different one, for which, compassionately, I saw the brotherhood pining in dire distress, scourging and mortifying their flesh. But who can know aright and clear the only true source of salvation?

Parsifal proclaimed that the religious should change their 'source'. Mortifying the flesh *(i.e., asceticism)* is also essentially egoistic, and so will not transform anyone. Afflicting the flesh does not resolve the desire for gratification; it is just another form of gratification. *Parsifal* proclaims that 'another', a different 'source' is the reservoir that can bring about transformation.

Kundry in wild ecstasy, and totally missing the point, inquires if it was her kiss that brought this revelation to Parsifal. Her *brute nature*, only further stimulated, probes that if her kiss achieved that, how much more her embrace would raise him to godhead:

KUNDRY
Redeem the world, if this is your destiny: make yourself a god for an hour, and for that let me be damned forever, my wound never be healed!

Kundry thus reveals that she too has a wound that never heals. As we stated in the previous chapter, *she is the wound that cannot be healed*. Parsifal again makes a profound statement:

PARSIFAL
Blasphemer! I offer you salvation!

How did she blaspheme? It was not about her desire to sexually unite with Parsifal. With Wagner's sleight-of-hand here, the symbolism is unveiled; she never believed her wound could be healed! This is the dilemma Wagner is addressing regarding religion and Enlightenment. Through his *Parsifal* he exposes that redemption occurs, *without* dogma or human reasoning, which espouses egoistic works or asceticism to attain Divinity. If religious dogma attained it or the disbelief in God provided it, then Amfortas and Kundry would have been healed long ago.

Kundry insists on having sex with Parsifal. Then Parsifal strikes at the heart of the matter:

PARSIFAL
Love and redemption shall be yours if you will show me the way to Amfortas.

What?!!! What does the path to Amfortas have to do with *her* redemption? She responds with the obvious retort - *NEVER!* She adds how she mocked him, that through her derision he fell prey to his own spear. Parsifal continues:

PARSIFAL
Who dared to wound him with the holy weapon?

KUNDRY
He - he! who once punished my laughter: his curse - ha! - gives me strength; I will call the weapon against you if you grant that sinner mercy! Ah, this is madness! -

Pity! Pity on me! Be mine for one hour! Let me be yours for one hour, and you shall be led on your way!

(She tries to embrace him. He thrusts her aside violently.)

PARSIFAL
Away, unholy woman!

KUNDRY
(starting up in wild fury and calling into the background.)

Help! Help! Here! Seize the scoundrel! Here! Bar his path! Bar his passage! And though you escape from here and find all the roads in the world, that road you seek, that path you shall not find, for any path and passage that leads you away from me I curse for you. Stray and be lost! You whom I know so well, I give him into your power!

KLINGSOR
(Has appeared on the rampart and wields a lance at Parsifal.)

Halt! I have the right weapon to fell you! The fool shall fall to me through his master's Spear!

(He hurls the Spear, which remains poised above Parsifal's head.)

PARSIFAL
(Seizing the Spear in his hand and holding it above his head.)

With this sign I rout your enchantment. As the Spear closes the wound which you dealt him with it, may it crush your lying splendor into mourning and ruin!

(He has swung the Spear in the sign of the Cross; the castle sinks as if by an earthquake. The garden swiftly withers to a desert; faded flowers are strewn on the ground. - Kundry falls to the ground with a scream).

(Parsifal pauses once more as he hastens away, and at the top of the ruined wall turns back to Kundry.)

PARSIFAL
You know where you can find me again!

(He hurries away. Kundry has raised herself a little and looks at him)

"PARSIFAL: THE WILL AND REDEMPTION"

PART 3: Transformation and Reformation

For the first time, Kundry has been unsuccessful in arousing the sensual desires of a male. She was in turmoil, which she called *madness*. Remember Parsifal's name and its meaning - it means not just *innocent fool* - it also means *madness*. Parsifal's Compassion (the Tree of Life) caused bewilderment to the Enlightenment in Kundry. She claimed that Klingsor, who had the Divine Spear, gave her strength, and she cursed Parsifal for wanting to show mercy to Amfortas. Within a breath of claiming strength and condemning Parsifal for showing mercy, she again asked for him to be united with her, if only for an hour.

For the same reason as Wagner saw Buddhism and Hinduism as flawed, Nietzsche found it acceptable. Nietzsche, being an avid believer in *natural selection,* saw Buddhism as empowering to Darwinism. From his *Anti-Christ,* "*Let anyone dare to speak to me of its 'humanitarian' blessings!*"[82] In that work, Nietzsche opposes Christianity because its benevolence interferes with natural selection. In the Buddhist/Hindu caste system, the weak and poor remain in their karmic condition and die, just like a weak species in Darwinian evolution. Nietzsche did not espouse Buddhism as his chosen path of spirituality; he thought that those of lesser race and intelligence would remain at their current lower status and then die, like Jews and Christians. However, when confronted by Compassion, which for Wagner is at the center of reality and connects humanity to the Divine, Nietzsche and those of like thought responded with vehemence. To Nietzsche, such a notion as Divine Compassion is contrary to the *laws of Nature*. In contrast, Wagner considered Germany, and for that matter Europe, on a road to savagery just because of such natural selection. He thought that to remove the Divine element, the Christian element of Christ's compassion, would leave us with a highly intellectualized cruelty. Sadly, with hindsight, we find Wagner spot on:

*"... the trouble of the constitution of the World is this: all steps in evolution of the utterances of Will, from the reaction of primary elements, through all the lower organizations, right up to the richest human intellect, stand side by side in space and time, and consequently the highest organism cannot but recognize itself and all its works **as founded on the Will's most brutal of manifestations.** ... So long as we have to fulfill the work of the Will, that Will which is ourselves, there in truth is nothing for us but the spirit of Negation, the spirit of our own will that, blind and hungering, can only plainly see itself in its un-will toward whatsoever crosses it, is as obstacle or disappointment. Yet that which crosses it, is but itself again: so that its rage expresses nothing save its self-negation: and **this self-knowledge can be gained at the last by Pity born of suffering** - which, cancelling the Will expresses the negation of a negative; and that by every rule of logic, amounts to Affirmation."*[83] *(bold added for emphasis)*

In relating the above statement to Klingsor and the evolving Enlightenment philosophy, Wagner was pointing out that without *self-knowledge gained by Pity (Compassion) born of suffering*, there is nothing left but *the Will's most brutal manifestations,* a self-seeking Will. Thus to this *self-seeking Will,* anything like compassion, humanitarianism, and other

"PARSIFAL: THE WILL AND REDEMPTION"

such qualities are seen as an obstacle or disappointment needing to be removed. This is why Kundry called for Klingsor's help. Parsifal's pity, born of Amfortas' suffering, and for that matter also born of Kundry's liberation, was seen as an obstacle. Klingsor's hurling the Sacred Spear at Parsifal was an attempt to remove the obstacle.

Similarly, Kundry called Amfortas *a sinner*, not just from a religious perspective, but also from her position of egoistic 'knowing' - *mocking disappointment*. In Klingsor's domain, she was of the so-called Enlightened, and scorned Amfortas' religious failure. Her earlier proclamation, *"... a sinner sinks into my arms! Then I laugh – laugh!"* for her was the heart of the matter. The sinners in her arms were none other than the Grail knights, who supposedly attained holiness and spiritual ascendancy. Yet they easily sank into her arms, only proving the weakness and frailty of their religion - hence she mockingly laughs!

This thinking justifies cruelty and excuses violence. Kundry called upon Klingsor to strike Parsifal with the stolen Spear. The Spear, the Divine quality of the *Will-to-Give*, the *Will-to-Redeem*, was thus misused to do just the opposite. It was meant to give Life, but once again was used to wound. To Klingsor, Parsifal is the obstacle. In contrast, at the beginning, Titurel was imposing ascendancy to godhood by removing obstacles of weakness, which in his case was the removal of Klingsor. Titurel attempted to protect godhood by enshrining it through religion; Klingsor wanted to attain godhood by denying and conquering the existence of God. In both cases what crosses the *self-seeking Will* is actually a manifestation of *itself again*. The one mirrors the other. This is the negation Wagner spoke of, *"Yet that which crosses it, is but itself again: so that its rage expresses nothing save its self-negation..."*.

The Spear, representing Creative Force, the *Will-to-Give*, the *Will-to-Create*, and most importantly, the *Will-to-*

Redeem, when in the hands of those who do not perceive or who deny the Divine, transform that *Will* into a destructive force. The result is the *Will-to-Take*, the *Will-to-Dominate*, the *Will-to-Survive*. To the 'natural' man, the so-called enlightened man, the notion of Divine Compassion, *Free-Will-Suffering* for redemption, is contrary to all that is natural. To the 'natural' man, compassion is against nature:

> *"To the natural man the reversal of the Will is certainly itself the greatest miracle, for it implies an abrogation of the laws of Nature; that which has effected it must consequently be far above Nature ... The very shape of the Divine had presented itself in anthropomorphic guise; it was the body of the quintessence of all pitying Love, stretched out upon the cross of pain and suffering. A symbol beckoning to the highest pity, to a worship of suffering, to an imitation of this breaking of all self-seeking Will: nay, a picture, a very effigy!"*[84]

Klingsor believed he could conquer the foolish Parsifal and hurled the Spear at him - violence. However, supernaturally, it stopped and hovered over Parsifal's head. Parsifal, formerly Siegfried, did not respond by violence; rather, he showed Compassion. Wagner skillfully combined Christianity and Buddhism, honing out their societal, cultural, and dogmatic 'imperfections', and combined them with Norse and Teutonic mythologies in *The Ring*.

Just as Kundry's kiss was pivotal, so too these events are pivotal, representing an intersection of Wagner's mythology and philosophy, as in a poem written by the Middle High German poet, Rudolf Von Ems, between 1230 and 1254 AD.[85] It was a Christian adaptation of the biography of Gautama Buddha, which was called, Barlaam, and Josaphat. It was widely distributed throughout medieval Europe. According to the legend, the king of India persecuted the Christian Church which was founded by the Apostle Thomas.

"PARSIFAL: THE WILL AND REDEMPTION"

However astrologers predicted that the king's son, Josaphat, would become a Christian. In fear, the king isolated his son from contact with the outside world. Regardless of the king's efforts, Josaphat met St. Barlaam and was converted to Christianity. The king tried in many ways to win back the young prince, but none of them were successful. The king then consulted with a sorcerer and sent him a beautiful woman. Upon meeting the woman, Josaphat attempted to convert her. While resisting her charms, she tells him:

> *"... if you want to save my soul, grant me one little request: sleep with me tonight, just once is all I ask, and I promise you I will become a Christian first thing tomorrow morning. For if, as you say, there is joy in heaven among the angels when a sinner repents, surely the one responsible for the conversion must be owed a special reward. Just do as I ask this once and you will win my salvation."*[86]

Josaphat rejects the woman's request and is attacked by demonic forces. He makes the sign of the Cross and the evil forces flee.

Of course, this sounds familiar; it is virtually identical to what Wagner penned in the conclusion of Act II. However, to help understand its full meaning, we will consider another intersection of Wagner's mythology and philosophy, in the story of Odin's eight-legged horse, Sleipnir. In an artistic depiction from the 9th Century AD, known as the Tjängvide image stone, Odin is brought home to Valhalla and a Valkyrie offers him greeting with a horn full of mead. With a cup in one hand and *his spear hovering over his head,* the dual nature of Odin as poet and warrior is revealed - his higher nature as a poet, and his lower nature as a warrior.[87]

In *The Ring*, the Spear was associated with Wotan. That symbolism was carried over to *Parsifal*, with Titurel, Amfortas, and Klingsor. Each in their own way tried to protect his interest, especially Amfortas who misused the Spear in an attempt to rid the world of evil, only to fall prey to the very forces he tried to overcome. In that moment, Parsifal had no desire to conquer anyone, only to redeem those who suffered. Odin's dual nature, as poet and warrior, is the dual nature of higher spirituality in contrast to lower brute nature. Because Parsifal didn't succumb to lower brute nature, the intended misuse of the Spear was not, and could not be fulfilled. Once thrown, it *had* to stop and hover over Parsifal's head. Regardless of Klingsor's intention, *the Spear immediately responded to its resemblance* (that 'resemblance' being Parsifal). In that moment Parsifal had no ego to take for himself; his 'lower' brute nature was overpowered, and his 'higher' Divine nature was revealed, the *Will-to-Give*. In the *Gospel of Matthew*, it says:

> "And he who does not take up his cross and follow Me [cleave steadfastly to Me, conforming wholly to My example in living and, if need be, in dying also] is not worthy of Me. Whoever finds his [lower] life will lose it [the higher life], and whoever loses his [lower] life on My account will find it [the higher life]."**88**

The Spear hovered over Parsifal revealing the unity of his higher nature. His lower and higher natures found semblance and cohesion - they became one. Parsifal, taking the Spear, made the sign of the Cross, the representation of his higher nature; or as Wagner stated, *"... the very effigy"*. Through this revelation of Parsifal's higher nature, Klingsor's realm was destroyed. What was once a colorful illusion of power and blossoming prosperity, but which was also an annihilation of belief in the Divine, became a desert. For Wagner, Enlightenment can be felled quickly in the face of true higher nature. While Enlightenment has all the façades of power, prosperity, and the uselessness of religion, its arrogance and therapy can be ended in an instant. *Brute nature*, regardless how intellectual it appears and of how it attempts rationalize itself, will always negate itself. Within sixty years a manifestation of that brute nature became

"PARSIFAL: THE WILL AND REDEMPTION"

manifest in both the Nazi and Communist systems, and in some of the great minds of the day, justifying genocide. Great minds when chained to brute nature can perpetrate great horrors.

Parsifal did not consider his victory complete with the destruction of Klingsor's domain, he also wanted to find the path back to Amfortas. His compassion moved him to heal Amfortas and to liberate the Grail. His final words here to Kundry were, *"You know where you can find me again".* Note that he said, *"... again".* Kundry was still being offered salvation, but not through her brute, sensual nature, or through some kind of natural evolution. Parsifal was telling her that if she wanted salvation, she could find it if she tried.

The curtain falls.

"EXPLORING RICHARD WAGNER'S FINAL TREATISE"

ACT III

"PARSIFAL: THE WILL AND REDEMPTION"

Part I: The Prodigals Return

The leitmotif that commences the third act Prelude is nothing less than the genius we experienced previously. Here to reveal the drama, we see a development of leitmotifs, intentional variations, and augmentations. The key signature is D^b, which is where the Redemption leitmotif concluded in *Götterdämmerung*. Evidently this key signature spoke redemptive resonance to Wagner. The first four notes of the Prelude are most interesting - they are the bells of Monsalvat, upturned. In the key of D^b, the bells would chime - B^b, E, F, B^b. Here in Act III, the Prelude begins with a low B^b, then F, then the higher B^b, concluding on the lower E. Musically, Wagner is telling us that something has changed or, better said, *transformed*. The entire first two phrases, with the first note of the third phrase, total eleven notes, sound warm and lovely. Later however, when we return to the Castle of the Grail, those same notes/leitmotif become the sinister processional of the knights and the funeral march of Titurel. Flashing forward to that moment, to its ominous tone, the knights say:

KNIGHTS (SECOND PROCESSION)
He whom you carry there, it's sinful Guardian.

KNIGHTS (FIRST PROCESSION)
We bear him today, because once more - for the last time - he will exercise the Office.

KNIGHTS (SECOND PROCESSION)
(Amfortas is now set down on the couch behind the altar of the Grail, the coffin [of Titurel] is placed in front; the knights turn towards him.)

Alas! Alas! Guardian of the Grail! For the last time! Be mindful of your charge!

From warm, lovely, and peaceful comfort, to sinister and judgmental condemnation (like the Tree of the Knowledge of Good and Evil from which it spawns), religion has its good points and, of course its bad ones. In the hands of the pious and egoistic, it has caused hideous holy wars and genocide. Wagner's point is evident, that the religious knowledge of good and evil, as its Tree, is a death sentence. But make no mistake, what was just destroyed in Act II, Klingsor and his illusions of grandeur, in being self-enlightened were as empty as the religion he did not believe in. Skepticism of the Divine in Enlightenment doctrine, and in its many child-doctrines (such as modern psychoanalysis) also have two sides, of good and evil. Wagner would say that, although many have been helped, healed and empowered by science, those with science in their grasp who do not perceive the Divine are no different than those who are what he calls 'religious' - with wars and genocide resulting. Whether religious or non-religious, we cannot escape our *brute nature*; it must be overcome - transformed into a higher, Divine reality.

A dictionary definition of religion is, *"relating to or manifesting faithful devotion to ... "*[89], and you can fill in the rest. Religious *worship* is more subtle - it can be of writings, a statue, a philosophy, a football team, a person, or even science. Religious worship, to Wagner, feeds the *Self-Will*, or *Ego*. The challenge in this final act of *Parsifal* is that the *Self-*

"PARSIFAL: THE WILL AND REDEMPTION"

Will does not think it has a problem. Wagner's point, to his contemporaries who he saw as worshipping themselves, their philosophies, and their sciences, was that *"... the spirit of our own will that, blind and hungering, can only plainly see itself in its un-will toward whatsoever crosses it, as an obstacle or disappointment"*. For Wagner, destroying Klingsor's castle was the first step towards his true enlightenment. Wagner thought the Enlightenment was just another form of religion, with another face, a reformed idol called humanism, stating *"God is dead"*[90], and thus just another manifestation of *Self-Will*. To destroy the notion that not perceiving the spiritual made a person more rational, self-controlled and prudent as a person, only opens the door to the inevitable - justifiable, clever *brute nature*. Wagner attempts to dismantle both religion and Enlightenment type philosophy, which have been around since the metaphorical day when Adam covered himself with a fig leaf, as quickly as he dismantled Klingsor.

Back to the beginning of Act III, as the warm Prelude progresses, we are reintroduced to the meadow where we began our journey in Act I. Because of Parsifal's actions, we saw Klingsor's flower-garden in Act II revert back to its original, desert landscape. As the curtain rises for this act we find ourselves back in the Meadow of the Grail but the landscape has changed a bit as well; we hear groaning from a thorny thicket. Flowers are in bloom amidst thorns and dry brush, and Kundry of course is among the thorns. Gurnemanz recognizes her voice and awakens her - she is stiff, like a corpse. Gurnemanz massages her limbs as her life slowly returns. The stage directions set the scene:

> *(When at last she opens her eyes, she utters a cry. Kundry is in the coarse robe of a penitent, similar to that in Act I, but her face is paler and the wildness has vanished from her look and behavior. - She gazes long at Gurnemanz. Then she rises, arranges her clothing and hair and at once sets to work like a serving-maid.)*

Things are altered. Kundry is wearing the same penitent clothing, but her appearance has changed. Gurnemanz asks her to say something, but she only motions, saying:

KUNDRY
(slowly bows her head: then hoarsely and brokenly brings out the words)

Serve ... serve!

Gurnemanz observes that she is moving differently. There is no longer any wildness in her. Like most of us, when inner transformation begins, we tend to keep to the old patterns of our lives, even though something is emerging. In the dilemma of the new breaking forth through the old, we begin to see things differently. Most of the time, we try to put the new with the old, but eventually the new will break open into a fresh perception of reality.

Remember, we are in a mystical land. Things are changing, but not because flowers are blooming, but because our perception is changing. Thus, we see what we could not see before, like a lens focusing and a light brightening in a dark land. Kundry is changed in her inner person, though she is still trying 'to serve' from the same religious mindset as in Act I. Yet, in spite of her external behavior, she sees differently. Thus, Kundry is the first to recognize something new, someone is coming, and she points him out to Gurnemanz. It is Parsifal in black armor.

This first segment of Act III is about transformation through compassion and forgiveness. Parsifal arrives in black armor, which for Wagner, black armor represents *Ego*, the *Will-to-Receive-for-Itself*. Parsifal thus shed his *Will* and became the humble agent of redemption he was always intended to be. Is Parsifal wearing black armor only to keep to the Parzival story by Eschenbach, or the earlier story by Troyes? Not exactly; Wagner has again used existing

"PARSIFAL: THE WILL AND REDEMPTION"

literature and myth, and intertwined and transformed it with his own message.

Parsifal is soon to shed his *Self-Will*, which we all also have, to reveal the Divine within. *Transformation consists of a progression of honest inner encounters leading finally to external manifestation of change.* Parsifal overpowered his egoistic craving through realizing the suffering of Kundry, Amfortas, and the Savior. Even though their suffering alone was not enough to accomplish his transformation, it was enough to act as a catalyst. In that moment, he also recognized his need and called upon the Redeemer. Parsifal did not 'sin' like Kundry and Amfortas, but he did call himself a sinner. What was his sin? The *Will-to-Receive-for-Himself*, or to put it another way, the *Self-Will* - in his case, his foolishness. To Wagner, and to the Christianity, Buddhism, and Kabbalah that influenced him, the *Selfish-Will* is like a shell that encases the true self. Thus, Parsifal removed his exterior armor to become who he really was.

Let us remind ourselves of what Wagner said regarding the progression of transformation:

"... this must first be revealed to us, and Jesus Christ must first be recognized and imitated by us."

Parsifal made the sign of the Cross to destroy Klingsor's magic Garden. Wagner was trying to tell us that this action was not just a Christian religious act, but part of Parsifal's surrender to Christ-like transformation. The power of the *Will-to-Redeem* demonstrated in Christ's *Free-Will-Suffering* on humanities behalf; is not found within the symbology of a cross made by a gesture - rather it was within the genuine act of compassion that was revealed in the crucifixion. The external expression of Parsifal making the Sign of the Cross with the Spear is an outward expression of his inward transformation. Parsifal was no longer the *Self-Willed* innocent fool, but that *Will*, transformed into the *Will-to-Redeem* - thus, the fool made wise through Compassion. As the Good Friday music will tell us, the suffering of the Savior was the ultimate act of compassion and forgiveness. This is not about Parsifal adapting a religion, but about his 'becoming'. As noted above in Wagner's words, it is about Christ being revealed to Parsifal, and then about Christ being recognized by him, and finally about Christ being imitated by him.

The words at the conclusion of the opera *"The Redeemer, Redeemed"* have been difficult to interpret for some. Is this a statement about Parsifal, or Christ (or both)? We will soon see. But, if Parsifal is truly imitating and emulating Christ, then we may not be able to tell the difference, which is the ultimate point. The focal desire of Christ is clearly stated prior to the crucifixion in His prayer:

"... that they all may be one, as You, Father, are in Me, and I in You; that they also may be one in Us ... And the glory which You gave Me I have given them, that they may be one just as We are one: I in them, and You in Me; that they may be made perfect in one, and that the world may know that You have sent Me, and have loved them as You have loved Me."[91]

Through Amfortas' and Kundry's suffering, Christ's Divine Compassion for humanity was revealed to Parsifal. In that revelation came a realization, which caused Parsifal to recognize the Divine nature within himself. If this so-called Sacred Stage Drama was only about self-denial, as some have proposed, it would have little meaning. Resisting the *Ego* is in itself insufficient. To deny the self or this world without acquiring something greater is nothing more than idiosyncratic suicide. Sadly, this is what many have seen in Wagner, as well as in his spiritual sources. Rather, it is about the denial of *Self-Will* in order to discover the Divine. The problem before us is that we tend to consider the *Self-Will*, the *Ego*, the *Will-to-Survive*, as being who we are. We tend to think that to give up these aspects of our being is to cease

"PARSIFAL: THE WILL AND REDEMPTION"

to exist. But by giving up the *Will-to-Survive* through *Free-Will-Suffering*, we open ourselves to the Divine within us - the *Will-to-Redeem*. Wagner referred to this scriptural concept when he wrote *Religion and Art*:

> "For it became him, for whom are all things, and through whom are all things, in bringing many sons unto glory, to make the author of their salvation perfect through sufferings."[92]

Parsifal's armor, as well as Kundry's penitent clothing are manifestations of the *Self-Will*. In *Parsifal* we observe the transformation and shedding of the *Will-to-Survive*, to reveal the *Will-to-Redeem*.

Because of his armor, Gurnemanz could not perceive who Parsifal was. When Parsifal first entered the Realm of the Grail, he came only with his bow and arrow, thinking himself a warrior. Now as a mature man, he comes in his armor and is perceived by others as a warrior, but initially appears to Gurnemanz as (still) being of a 'lower' nature:

GURNEMANZ
Who there is approaching the holy spring, in dark attire of war?

That is none of the brethren!

Thus, he presented as a total stranger. He was not familiar to Gurnemanz, who decided at that point that this stranger did not belong in the realm. Is it not interesting that the one marked to bring salvation, is a stranger to the realm that proclaims it? Hence, religion strikes again!

Kundry, after pausing briefly to notice the newcomer, returned to 'serving' - to filling her pitcher with water. Parsifal appeared hesitant and dazed. He seated himself on a mound near the spring. Gurnemanz, after looking at Parsifal for a long time, approached the black knight. He asked him several questions to which Parsifal only shook his head. As in Act I, Gurnemanz quickly becomes agitated. In spite of his 'wisdom', his own religiosity emerged demanding that Parsifal lay down his weapons for fear of offending God. Take note again, the one who is closest to God-likeness here was being asked to change because of a concern for offending God. Wagner once again has revealed a polarizing dynamic; religiosity sees only the external, not the inward condition.

Without saying a word, Parsifal thrust the Spear into the ground, took off his helmet and laid down his weapons. He kneeled before the Spear and prayed. Gurnemanz then recognized him as the fool from long ago. He called to Kundry who confirmed this with a silent nod. He then recognized the Spear, and was elated.

By different paths, the two prodigals returned to the Realm of the Grail. Parsifal said nothing, and Kundry said only *"Serve";* she communicated by nods and gazes. Why? Like Parsifal, her *Will* changed. She no longer responded to the external world as she did before. She was now contemplative, with an emerging inner peace. The stage direction says, *"Kundry gazes steadily, but calmly at Parsifal".* Parsifal's choice was to yield to the Tree of the Knowledge of Good and Evil, or to invest in the Tree of Life. He chose Life. His emergence to Life was from an egoistic, ignorant *Self-Will;* hers was from egoistic, arrogant *Self-Will* of Enlightenment and religious dogma; from the Tree of the Knowledge of Good and Evil to the Tree of Life. Parsifal (as far as religion and Enlightenment philosophy was concerned) was the fool, who now emerged wise, 'knowing' Divine Life and emulating divinity. Kundry on the other hand was religiously and philosophically wise, knowing good and evil. However now she is being transformed into what the world would call foolish, to emerge wise, 'knowing' Divine Life and emulating divinity.

In Klingsor's castle, her self-centered Enlightenment and religious illusions were destroyed. Here she sheds her

"PARSIFAL: THE WILL AND REDEMPTION"

religiosity and discovers her true self. Both of them are discovering the *Will-to-Redeem*:

> "... the root here was necessarily found in a birth that issued, not from the 'Will-to-Live', but from the 'Will-to-Redeem'."

Wagner has written extensively on this concept. We suffer because of our *Will-to-Live*, or as he also calls it, the *Will-to-Survive*. When we discover Christ-like-Compassion, the *Will-to-Redeem*, we no longer suffer for the same reasons as before. The *Will-to-Live* will do whatever is necessary to enslave creation and to ensure survival of its self. However, when such a *Will* is removed, the *Will-to-Redeem*, the *Will-to-Bestow-the-Divine* has the opportunity to be revealed. This Divine *Will* sees itself as a part of all creation. Therefore to harm any part of it would be to destroy all of it.

Parsifal rose from his prayer and extended a hand of greeting to Gurnemanz:

PARSIFAL
Through error and the path of suffering I came; am I to believe myself wrested from it, now that I hear again the noise of the forest and greet you anew, good old man? Or do I still err? Everything seems changed.

GURNEMANZ
But tell me, to whom were you seeking the way?

PARSIFAL
To him who's deep lamenting I once heard in foolish wonder, to bring him salvation I dare think myself ordained.

But ah! An evil curse drove me about in trackless wandering, never to find the way to healing; numberless dangers, battles and conflicts forced me from my path even when I thought I knew it. Then I was forced to despair of holding unsullied the treasure to defend and guard which I earned wounds from every weapon; for I dared not wield this itself in conflict; unprofaned I have borne it beside me and now bring it home, gleaming clean and bright before you, the holy Spear of the Grail.

Parsifal asks, *"... do I still err? Everything seems changed"*. Though Parsifal has not erred in his awareness, everything *is* changing, and *he* is the agent of it. In Parsifal's explanation of his journey, he mentions that he never used the Spear in combat, unlike Klingsor used the power of the Spear *(the Will-to-Give)* to inflict pain. Parsifal recognized, or better said, became, the spiritual quality of the Spear, the *Will-to-Redeem*. Remember, this is why the Spear flung by Klingsor hovered over his head. Parsifal shed his *Self-Will*, and became *Free-Will-Suffering*. His sole purpose was then to find Amfortas and the Grail, and to return (or *give)* the Spear to its rightful place.

Unlike the squires at the beginning of our drama, Parsifal had no delusions of grandeur or of being venerated for his heroic deeds. Rather his motivation, at first through youthful egoistic ignorance, was now through sincere compassion. In a sense, his youthful foolishness aided his discovery of the Divine, and not a superior intellectualism. This is the point Wagner was making to his former friend Nietzsche, and to his contemporaries. Thus, the path to the Divine is what the Enlightenment would call foolishness, and what the blind faith of religion would not recognize.

His path back to Monsalvat, though laced with trials and hindrances, refined and opened a Divine Likeness in Parsifal. In Parsifal the youth, his egoistic *Self-Will* was not a shell he wore - it was integrated in his person. Now he enters with his *Ego, Will-to-Survive*, only as an outer shell, as armor, and soon he will remove even that so only the reality of his transformation will remain.

Another perspective on Wagner's referring to armor as the *Ego*, the *Self-Will*, is that we use it both to protect, and to

"PARSIFAL: THE WILL AND REDEMPTION"

take pride in ourselves. It protects us from pain caused by others - the lances thrown by others. *Ego* can also help us look menacing so others will not get too close, a form of protection; but it can prevent others from seeing who we really are down deep, only showing what egoistic personas we choose to reveal. Another aspect of the armor we wear is that we polish it and keep it shiny so others can see our accomplishments and triumphs. Therefore, as Wagner pointed out, it is so hard to rid ourselves of the contradiction. The *Self-Will*, whether religious or so-called intellectually enlightened, is not our true identity/reality. Unfortunately, the general condition of humanity is that we tend to be preoccupied with armor of egoistic identity, rather than of the true divinity of which we are a reflection and are destined to be.

To complete transformation, the armor must be shed. How does this happen? Through the development of Desire, or the appropriate *Will-to-Receive*. It must be a *Will-to-Receive* for the sake of the *Will-to-Give*; *Free-Will-Suffering* merges these two concepts, and together they become the *Will-to-Redeem*. This is portrayed by Parsifal freely returning, or compassionately *bestowing* the Spear; he emulates the Divine Masculine quality that has been missing. By returning the Spear, the revelation of Divinity is complete; the Spear and the Grail, the masculine and feminine attributes of God, are reunited, and to Wagner, God is revealed.

In the first chapter we described the hardship of attending the Festival in Wagner's time; that journey - in a sense - a journey before the journey - is often difficult even today for many who travel from afar to attend. This journey before the journey is what creates the necessary anticipation, which enlarges our desire for what is ahead. We also discussed in the first chapter why Wagner confined his works to Bayreuth. Most importantly, he intended that such a work as *Parsifal* must not be associated with the frivolity of a mere entertainment, but he also wanted his audience to become initiates in the experience. In other words, he was attempting to engender in his audience a *desire* for the message contained within the opera. For Wagner, his theater and in particular this Sacred Stage Drama, was serious business.

Between Acts II and III, while we, the initiated, discuss what we see over a sausage-on-a-roll and an Aktien Pils, Parsifal is faced with trials and challenges. Each challenge will afford him the choice of quitting, or pressing through. In that moment of decision, *desire* will be formed in Parsifal to transform. His *Self-Will*, his *desire,* his inner ability, the *Will-to-Receive* must be developed enough to successfully transform. By developing that desire, we too are metaphorically adding substance to our own inner Grail (the Divine Feminine). If we can develop the desire, we then can receive that which only the Spear, the Divine Masculine, opens to us - the issuing forth of Life and Divine Likeness.

Thus, religion in this context is no different from the egoism found in Klingsor's Garden. Religion does not necessarily create a selfless desire to reveal the Divine, it only increases the *Self-Will* of the Tree of the Knowledge of Good and Evil. Thus, Kundry in Act I 'served' for acceptance and approval; Titurel would afflict his son, Amfortas, with the duty to perform the office, which only enforced his torment; and the knights (and squires) had an oppressive caste system. But in Act III, for Parsifal, ignorant awareness of another's suffering has developed into compassion, in concert with a congruent selfless-desire, resulting in an emergent revelation of the Divine. We could say that what was developing within Parsifal had become too large for his outer-shell, his *Self-Will*, the armor he wore. Thus, with the aid of the Spear he (re)found Monsalvat, and was easily able to remove his dark armor. Note - dark armor, not (knight-in-shining) armor. Gurnemanz, still seeing through 'natural' eyes, is overjoyed at the sight of the Spear. He yet did not yet see, but was gradually becoming aware that Parsifal was transforming to the spiritual quality of the Spear:

"PARSIFAL: THE WILL AND REDEMPTION"

GURNEMANZ
Here you are: this is the Domain of the Grail whose brotherhood awaits you. Ah, it needs the salvation, the salvation - that you bring! ...

Amfortas, striving against his wound, brought agony to his soul, in angry defiance desires only death. No entreaties, no misery of his knights moves him to perform again his holy office. The Grail has long lain locked in the shrine; thus its guardian, repentant of his sin, hopes to hasten his end, since he cannot die while he beholds it, and with his life, to end his agony. The divine supply is now denied us, and common food must sustain us; our heroes' strength is parched. Never messages come to us any more, calls from a distance to holy war; our miserable and leaderless knighthood staggers about, pale and woeful. In this corner of the forest I myself hide, silently awaiting death to which my aged warrior lord surrendered. For Titurel, my holy hero, whom the sight of the Grail no longer refreshed, is dead - a man like all men!

Hearing this, Parsifal springs to his feet with tremendous grief. He accuses himself of causing all this suffering because of his blindness:

PARSIFAL
... my foolish head have borne from eternity, since no repentance, no atonement can free me of my blindness; though I was appointed for deliverance, the last path of deliverance escapes me, lost I am in hopeless error!

Parsifal is not to be blamed for Amfortas' choices or Titurel's death, but he does feel responsible thinking that if he had arrived sooner and had overcome the difficulties in finding the path, things would have been different. This is known as counterfactual thinking, which is known to have a poor outcome clinically - it doesn't work well. He doubts that he can complete his journey. While true that he has not yet attained the Divine, so to speak, whatever remains to be done has not delayed his arrival at Monsalvat. If anything, Parsifal has arrived when he was supposed to have arrived. Titurel died, but his death was necessary for Divinity to be revealed (once again). In other words, religious tradition had to die because it concealed the Divine. This final act of the drama, and for that matter of all of Wagner's works, are intended to open to us that notion.

Gurnemanz leads Parsifal to the nearby spring and refreshes him. He encourages him to go to the castle, especially for Titurel's funeral. It is interesting to note that Titurel died when Klingsor was destroyed. As we stated before, everything in this domain is connected; they represented one spiritual quality, with two personas.

Parsifal sensed not so much his own failure to arrive sooner, but the additional guilt suffered by Amfortas. Not only was Amfortas tormented by his wound and how he obtained it; but in wanting to end his suffering and by keeping the Grail covered, he thinks he hastened or caused his father's death. Amfortas' guilt was compounded!

When Gurnemanz finishes refreshing Parsifal, Kundry kneels by the spring, takes some water and washes Parsifal's feet. He looks at her with peaceful wonder and asks Gurnemanz to bathe his head as well. Gurnemanz sprinkles water on Parsifal's head, like a baptism. While he is doing this, Kundry reaches into her garment and takes a golden phial. She opens it and pours some if it on Parsifal's feet. She then dries his feet with her hair. This is a very powerful scene, and is of course a direct reference to what Mary Magdalene did to Christ, as per the Gospel of John. Some Biblical historians also refer to her as Mary of Bethany, Sister of Martha and Lazarus:

"Then he turned to the woman and said to Simon, 'Look at this woman kneeling here. When I entered your home, you didn't offer me water to wash

"PARSIFAL: THE WILL AND REDEMPTION"

the dust from my feet, but she has washed them with her tears and wiped them with her hair. You didn't greet me with a kiss, but from the time I first came in, she has not stopped kissing my feet. You neglected the courtesy of olive oil to anoint my head, but she has anointed my feet with rare perfume. I tell you, her sins - and they are many - have been forgiven, so she has shown me much love."[93]

Wagner's reference here to the New Testament is direct and has several ramifications. The anointing of one's feet speaks volumes. First, to be anointed is to be anointed with oil for the journey ahead, and anointing with oil represents the Holy Spirit[94]. It also represents anointing as one is being prepared for burial. Lastly, and most important, for Kundry it represents genuine repentance and the transformation to Divine Life. Regarding the last point, Jesus said, *"... her sins - and they are many - have been forgiven, so she has shown me much love"*. Kundry's days of serving to expiate her sins in this moment have ended. Why? Because serving to expiate sin or to atone for it, is still the *Will-to-Survive*, it is egoism masked in religious piety. Here she is faced with surrendering her *Self-Will*, and simply accepting her forgiveness which is and has always been, freely offered:

GURNEMANZ
Pure of heart! Compassionate sufferer, enlightened healer! As you have endured the sufferings of the redeemed, lift the last burden from his head!

Gurnemanz prays to God as he baptizes Parsifal, to lift this final burden of grief. He appeals to Christ as being one who endured the sufferings of the redeemed and equates Parsifal's journey to that of Christ. In response, Parsifal scoops water from the spring and baptizes Kundry:

PARSIFAL
My first duty I so perform: Receive this baptism, and believe in the Redeemer!

(Kundry lowers her head to the earth and seems to weep violently.)

(Parsifal turns and looks with gentle rapture on forest and meadow, which are now glowing in the morning light.)

How beautiful seem the meadows today! Once I came upon magic flowers which twined their tainted tendrils to my head; but never did I see so mild and tender the grass, the blossoms and flowers, nor did they smell so sweet nor speak to me with such tender love.

Profound and yet so simple! Kundry is forgiven. No penitent deeds or pious works could attain this; this is where true faith comes in. It is not a faith that believes in what it cannot see; it is a faith that accepts forgiveness and recognizes that there is nothing the *Self-Will* can do to obtain it. It is a faith that accepts what the Redeemer freely bestows. It is the *Free Will-of-Receiving* that is being offered. It is the *Will-to-Receive-for-Itself*, transformed into the *Will-to-Receive-to-Give*. By freely accepting the Redeemer's love and forgiveness, we *give* Him pleasure by receiving what He offers. It's like a person that provides a lavish dinner to bless and bring joy to the receiver. For the receiver to truly give pleasure to the Giver, that pleasure would not come in a form of repayment, or through sincere platitudes of gratitude. Rather, to truly bring joy to the Giver (especially since the Giver is Divine and His benevolence can never be repaid by anything in our power), the greatest gift we can give is to joyously receive.

This was not a request for Kundry to believe in God. Rather, she was being asked to believe, and receive/understand that she was forgiven, which for many is even more difficult than believing in God. In that moment Kundry wept traumatically. What she had long awaited came to pass. Her transformation was within the simplicity of acceptance, not the complexity of egoistic religious works. This is the point Wagner was making:

> *"Now we may assume that if belief in Jesus had remained the possession of these 'poor' alone, the Christian dogma would have passed to us as the simplest of religions."* [95]

Kundry weeps. In that moment, Wagner changes the key signature to *C major* for only three measures. The cellos and double-bass play a *low G* pizzicato five times with interval rests, followed by one more on the double-bass, a *B natural* representing the droplets of Kundry's tears. Immediately, Parsifal notices the forest and the meadow, upon which morning light is dawning, at which point the unforgettable Good Friday music begins. He equates the blossoming flowers to his past experience with the flower-maidens of Klingsor's magic Garden. These flowers are blossoming with a different gentle sweetness compared to the seductions of the past. Gurnemanz tells Parsifal that it is the light of Good Friday. Parsifal cries out, calling it the day of the greatest grief! While that was true, that day gave birth to something greater than the suffering of the Savior:

GURNEMANZ
You see that is not so. It is the tears of repentant sinners that today fall as holy dew on the field and meadow; thus making them flourish. Now all creation rejoices at the Savior's sign of love and dedicates to Him its prayer. No more can they see Him on the Cross; they look instead up to man redeemed, who feels freed from the burden of sin and horror, made clean and whole through God's loving sacrifice. Now grass and flowers in the meadows know that the foot of man will not tread them down today, but that, as God with divine patience that is his mercy which has suffered for him, so man today in devout grace will protect with a gentle step. Thus all creation gives thanks and all that

blooms soon dies, nature is absolved from sin today in its day of innocence.

Wagner, again merging aspects of Christianity and Buddhism, connects the Savior's crucifixion not only with the salvation of mankind, but also with nature. While the New Testament speaks pointedly of this,[96] Buddhism emphasizes the connection in a broader way.[97] Wagner embraces both. Kundry's connection to nature is that her tears water the earth. Parsifal says that her tears are the dew of blessing that makes the meadow smile - and that makes us smile.

We stated earlier, in the chapter on the first part of Act I - *The Domain of Religion*, that Kundry in affect was the wound that could not be healed. We expounded that she could not be healed because of her self-condemnation of her mockery of Christ. Though she worked in a penitent manner, she was the lowest in the caste system of the knights, and many times the brunt of their jokes. It was as if, because she mocked, she was mocked. She vacillated from doing religious works to gain acceptance, to the rejection of that behavior when under the influence of Klingsor. There she abandoned religious dogma and became the agent of late-Enlightenment philosophy that did not acknowledge the Divine as anything more than a force of nature, at best.

At the conclusion of Act II, we saw Wagner destroying Enlightenment philosophical beliefs, but not with the intention of celebrating religious ones. One thing the early Enlightenment did espouse, in the 17th Century, was simplicity, and so did Wagner. However, in the long view, as Enlightenment evolved through the Industrial Revolution, though still claiming simplicity, it was no longer simple. Both the Enlightenment, and the religion of that time were weighed down with complexities of what the human ego, the *Self-Will*, espoused. The Cross of Christ, which Wagner addresses in each act represents *Selfless-Will*, the *Will-to-Redeem*, not only humanity, but all of nature. God the Creator, through His

"PARSIFAL: THE WILL AND REDEMPTION"

selfless act, redeems the Creation. For Wagner, Christ as Savior, the Cross and the Divine Compassion it represents, was not merely the force of nature in an involuntary evolutionary vigor, but the Life source of all nature. It is why the Creation exists in the first place - because of Divine Love. To deny that in philosophy, in belief and most importantly in practice, was to destroy oneself.

Parsifal reached gently for Kundry and kissed her on the forehead. Consider the contrast to Kundry's seductive kiss in Klingsor's Garden, which brought Parsifal awareness of Amfortas' and her sins and suffering. Here Parsifal kissed Kundry and it brought her awareness, a new 'knowing', one of wholeness through compassionate forgiveness. Two kisses, two people, though *"Wills"* apart; the first in Klingsor's Garden, the *Will-to-Receive-for-Itself;* the second in the Meadow of the Grail, *the Will-to-Give* born of compassion.

Here Kundry finally left the realm of the Knowledge of Good and Evil, and entered the realm of the Tree of Life. She had to give up atoning for herself to earn merit with God, and in contrast to simply receive the offered compassion. In other words, she had to free herself from her religion, whose source is *Self-Willed* arrogance, the Serpent in the Tree, and accept that she was truly released from her inner debt.

"EXPLORING RICHARD WAGNER'S FINAL TREATISE"

PART 2: THE DIVINE REVEALED

The bells of Monsalvat ring in the distance. Recalling the conclusion of the second act, Parsifal asked Kundry to show him the way to Amfortas. Kundry responded, menacingly:

KUNDRY
... that road you seek, that path you will not find, for any path and way that leads you away from me, I curse for you!

Parsifal had just recently said to Gurnemanz, *"... the last path of deliverance escapes me ..."*. Was it because of Kundry's curse? Or was it because the Divine Masculine must first join with the Divine Feminine? It is the latter; in her deluded state, Kundry had been saying that any path that led Parsifal away from her was cursed. Again, truth concealed in lie, but she was in a sense correct - Parsifal was not going to find his way to Amfortas unless he found her first. In her broken, *Self-Willed* state at that time, she was only able to curse his path. Now that she was transforming, the 'path' to Kundry was clearing, and after that Parsifal could find his way to Amfortas. Now, rather than cursing Parsifal's path, she anoints his feet! Together through their transformations they are making their way to Amfortas, and to the union of both Grail and Spear, which was previously inaccessible.

The *Verwandlungsmusik* (Transformation Music) again begins. We are reminded that where we are now, and where we are going is a realm where time becomes space. Note the stage directions as the transformation progresses:

GURNEMANZ
Midday: the hour has come. My lord, permit your servant to guide you!

(Gurnemanz has brought out his mantle of the knights of the Grail, and he and Kundry place it on Parsifal. Parsifal solemnly takes up the Spear and with Kundry, follows Gurnemanz who slowly leads the way. - The scene very gradually changes, as in Act I, but from right to left. After remaining visible for a time the three disappear completely from sight as the forest gradually vanishes and rocky vaults draw near in its place. In the vaulted passages the sound of bells increasingly grow in intensity. The rocky walls open disclosing once more, as in Act I, the great hall of the Grail, but without the festival tables. Dim lighting. From one side enter knights bearing Titurel's body in a coffin, from the other those carrying Amfortas on a litter, preceded by the covered shrine with the Grail.)

Here Gurnemanz adorns Parsifal with his 'garment of the Grail knights', which Parsifal receives without the usual ritual rites or indoctrination. Why the 'short service'? - because rites and indoctrination cannot replace inner transformation. Even though they may symbolically show what transformation could look like, they do not replace the experience of it. For religion, ritual, doctrine and their symbols alone are sufficient. Let us remind ourselves what we stated Wagner said at the beginning of this book, *"Religion has sunk into an artificial life, when she finds herself compelled to keep on adding to the edifice of her dogmatic symbols, and thus conceals the one divinely True ..."*. Note the phrase: *"... conceals the one divinely True ..."*. Through *Parsifal*, Wagner is telling us that for spirituality, the transformation *is* or *becomes* accomplished *through* our inner journey and discovery - the rituals are life's encounters, the symbols are inner meaning found within those experiences, and the doctrine is born, as it were on the road to itself.

Before we continue with our discussion of Act III, we would like to briefly chronicle and describe some of the events that occurred at this point in the drama, in August of 1882 during the final performance of *Parsifal* in Wagner's lifetime (of course, at Bayreuth):

Hermann Levi, now a friend of the Wagner's for over a year and his first conductor of *Parsifal*, recounts:

> *"During the transformation music in the third act, the Master came into the orchestra pit, up to my desk took the baton from my hand and conducted the performance to its conclusion."*[98]

Did Wagner know that this would be the final time he would see his beloved Bayreuth Festival? Did he know that this was his farewell performance of his farewell composition? It was less than a year before Wagner would breathe his last.

Setting the stage, as it were for these events, Wagner was dealing with his most recent set of problems. As we mentioned earlier, in February of 1881 he published an essay which appeared in the *Bayreuther Blätter,* criticizing and repudiating the anti-Semitism[99] rampant in Germany at that time, and he appears to have wanted to distance himself from it. This did not sit well with the anti-Semitic movement of the day who benefitted from apparent support by such a prominent personality as Wagner. His previous publications (most prominently, *Das Judenthum in der Musik*, September 1850) fueled their belief that he did support them, and so increased their interest in opposing his retraction.

Further, Wagner intentionally hired a Jew, Hermann Levi to conduct his sacred work. How could this espoused anti-Semite do such a thing? Some say that King Ludwig forced him to hire Levi, though there is no correspondence or any strong validation to support that claim[100]. Yet even if King Ludwig did force or encourage him to hire Levi, Wagner's resistance was not simply, or was not just based on Levi being Jewish. Hermann Levi was only one of many Jews who had participated in performances of Wagner's operas, or worked for or with Wagner in the past, including Angelo Neumann, Joseph Rubinstein (who actually lived with the Wagners), and others. Wagner probably still did see Jews, in some sense as 'less', but his convictions, supported by his writings also cannot be discounted.

The Christianity he was espousing was an additional factor to be considered. Although Wagner was, at least initially anti-Semitic, he also appears to have believed, at what was to be the end of his life that whether you are a Jew or Gentile, that not just in religion, but in *race* as well, all were redeemable. In a sense, Wagner may have been on his own journey which for him, as for his characters, was evolutionary. Some of his old baggage, or armor, may not yet have completely fallen away. It is interesting that he had his fill of revolution in his early life, but it seems that he was not finished with evolution. His views on religion and Christianity may have acted as the fulcrum on which balanced what appear to have been his changing views on anti-Semitism.

Since 325 AD, when Constantine decreed that the Jews were a *"detestable"* people,[101] and that so-called Christians should have nothing to do with them, what came to be known as anti-Semitism has been an official, decreed part of the neo-Christian European world. As recorded by Josephus and other historians, even prior to that time, Rome had an anti-Semitic posture toward Jews[102], even though Christians in general, prior to Constantine founded their faith on what is commonly now called the Old Testament, just like the Jews, as their Holy Scripture. While they regarded the writings of the Apostles as scripture as well, their writings were not officially canonized

"PARSIFAL: THE WILL AND REDEMPTION"

till 170 AD (Muratorian Cannon) and then reconsidered and restructured after Constantine in 363 AD at the council of Laodicea. Constantine had based his decree against Jews not only on the basis of pre-existing anti-Jewish Roman sentiment, but also on the basis of the writings of Tertullian, known as the 'Father of Latin Christianity', who wrote, *".... apart from the question of age, we neither accord with the Jews in their peculiarities in regard to food, nor in their sacred days, nor even in their well-known bodily sign, nor in the possession of a common name, which surely behoved to be the case if we did homage to the same God as they."*[103] This is the same Tertullian who wrote the horrible decrees about women we mentioned earlier when discussing Act II.

Within a hundred years of that initial decree, Constantius II and Theodosius escalated their decrees from Constantine's *"detestable"*, to *"sentence of death"*[104]. As developed and described in James Carroll's book, *Constantine's Sword* (Mariner Books, 2002), the following thousand-plus years would see much more of the same, politically as well as theologically. After all, the two perspectives were really one; to the Holy Roman Empire, allegiance to its version of Christianity was also an issue of national security. The Church espoused the idea that the Jews were the cause of Christ's death, and that the God of the Israelites was an angry, judgmental deity. They could not go too far in that direction officially, however, since the Israelite God was also two-thirds of their own Holy Trinity.

Even after the Reformation anti-Semitism remained rampant, as it still is in some parts of the world today. Consider Martin Luther's pamphlet from 1543 AD, *Von den Jüden und iren Lügen (On the Jews and their Lies)* in which he claims that the Jews are *"... full of the devil's feces ..."*. During the Nürnberg rallies, the Nazis actually displayed this pamphlet.

Darwinism in the 19th Century contributed to European anti-Semitism. As that it intensified, it also changed; religious aspects were de-emphasized, and race issues were emphasized. It became apparent that although one can change religion, one cannot change race. As mentioned earlier, Nietzsche considered Buddhism to be not so much a religion as a caste system based in survival of the fittest. Hence, emerging anti-Semitism was race-based, and there were those who explored and supported Darwinism to validate their anti-Semitic views.

Wagner diverged here from others with Darwinistic and other anti-Semitic views. It was not that he disagreed with the then-current context of anti-Semitism as being religion- or race-based, but that he was convinced that all races, including the Jews, were redeemable. He thought that the anti-Semitic movement was shifting toward barbarism. Hence, during the construction and opening of Bayreuth, Wagner became a vegetarian because he believed that eating animal flesh led to degeneration of the human race, and to the empowerment of *brute nature.* He thought and wrote that a natural vegetarian diet would promote a healthier humanity and rejuvenation toward our higher cognizance. Also, at that time he asserted regularly partaking of Holy Communion, through which *"even the most degenerate of races could be restored"*[105].

Thus, for Hermann Levi to conduct his Bayreuth performances of *Parsifal* was totally acceptable to Wagner; he was a friend as well as an employee. Nonetheless, these events did not go unnoticed by the anti-Semitic movement - the movement that Wagner snubbed by not signing Bernhard Förster's[106] 1880 petition addressed to Prince Bismarck demanding emergency laws against the Jews. Soon Wagner received an anonymous letter claiming that Cosima was having a sexual affair with Levi. Learning of this, in panic, Levi fled in fear. In a letter to Levi dated July 1, 1881, Wagner wrote:

"PARSIFAL: THE WILL AND REDEMPTION"

> "Much as I respect all your feelings, you are not making things easy either for yourself or us! What could so easily inhibit us in our dealing with you is the fact that you are always so gloomy and introspective! We are entirely at one in thinking that the whole world should be told about this, though what this means is that you must stop running away from us, thereby allowing such stupid suspicions to arise. For God's sake come back at once, and get to know us properly! You do not need to lose any of your faith, but merely to acquire the courage of your convictions! Perhaps some great changes about to take place in your life - but in all of events - you are my Parsifal conductor!"[107]

What an interesting statement - *"You do not need to lose any of your faith, but merely to acquire the courage of your convictions!"* You would think that because of what Wagner wrote in the past, he would demand the opposite. But to the contrary, Wagner was a man of his word to Levi. When Levi finally returned, he wrote the following during *Parsifal* rehearsals in 1882 regarding his connection and stay with the Wagners, keeping in mind he would conduct *Parsifal* for a total of twelve more years:

> "The rehearsals are in full swing and promise a performance such as never before. You can imagine how anxious I was until the cast was finally chosen and the Master had expressed his approval. The orchestra is thrilling - 32 violins, 12 cellos, 12 violas. The chorus is also good. For this entire week we are rehearsing the first act. This evening is the first full rehearsal with action. The Wagners are so good to me that I am constantly moved."

In addition, he wrote to his father, who was a rabbi, before Wagner's death:

> "You certainly could and you should like Wagner. He is the best and noblest of men. Of course

our contemporaries misunderstand and slander him. It is the duty of the world to darken those who shine. Goethe did not fare any better. That he bears no petty anti-Semitism like a country squire or a protestant bigot is seen by the way he treats me, Rubinstein, the late Tausig whom he loved dearly ... Even his fight against what he calls "Jewishness" in music and modern literature springs from the noblest of motives. I am convinced that posterity will learn what we who are close to him know already: that in him we had just as great a man as a musician. I consider myself very lucky to be working with such a man and I thank God for it every day." [108]

But what of Wagner's statement at the end of his letter to Levi, *"Perhaps some great changes about to take place in your life ...".* We will reserve comment on that until a little later in this chapter.

Returning now to our discussion of the conclusion of *Parsifal*, we left off when the procession onto the stage was being led by Gurnemanz, with Parsifal and Kundry following, together. Unlike Act I, where stage action was from left to right, here it was right to left, again emphasizing that things have changed. After passing through the castle vaults, all arrive in the Hall of the Grail - however, now it is dimly lit and there are no feasting tables. Titurel's coffin is carried in from one side, and Amfortas is carried in on his sickbed from the other side.

Once the group arrives in the Hall of the Grail for this transformation scene, an opening statement by the first procession of knights brings us up to date:

FIRST PROCESSION
(With the Grail and Amfortas)

In its protective shrine we carry the Grail to this holy office; whom do you carry in that dark shrine and bear in such sorrow?

"PARSIFAL: THE WILL AND REDEMPTION"

"In its protective shrine ..." are the first words here. Again echoing Wagner's words, *"... if Man made a law to shackle love ... he sinned against the law of his own existence, and therewith slew himself ...".*

Titurel did actually, effectively slay himself. He created the castle to protect the relics. By protecting them, he shackled them. He recruited the knighthood not only to serve the Grail, but also to protect it. One of those protecting knights was Klingsor. Rather than Titurel freely offering the forgiveness and compassion that the Grail could bestow to all, he banned Klingsor because of his imperfections. Thus, Titurel shackled Love. Klingsor in his desperation lost faith, and his remedy was to conquer the Knights of the Grail, to prove Titurel a failure, and to acquire the relics. To conquer and possess both the Spear and the Grail would be proof that the Divine did not exist, and that what Titurel served was nothing more than a powerless religion - it would be to conquer God. Finally, as Titurel aged he brought forth a son, Amfortas. In keeping with his father's zeal, he took the sacred Spear, the Divine *Will-to-Give*, but only to inflict further condemnation on Klingsor. Needless to say, Amfortas' plan did not work, and he fell prey to Klingsor. The result was a wound that wouldn't heal. Amfortas, in excruciating, continuous torment, was at an impasse. To reveal the Grail and continue in his office as king-priest would only serve to keep him alive in torment, with no cure. However, to conceal the Grail and to desire his own death would also mean death to Titurel, who at his advanced age needed the Grail to stay alive. Amfortas chose to conceal the Grail and hope for his own death, and thus his aged father died from no longer being able to behold the Grail. The sequence of events which Titurel began by desiring to protect the Grail, ended in his demise - thus, *"... therewith he slew himself".*

The knights continued to herald their *Self-Willed* woes against Amfortas:

SECOND PROCESSION
(with Titurel's body)

Within the memorial shrine lies the hero with the holy power, whom God Himself once took as His guardian: we have Titurel.

FIRST PROCESSION
Who did slay him that, in God's care, once guarded God Himself?

SECOND PROCESSION
The conquering burden of years slew him, since he could no longer look upon the Grail.

FIRST PROCESSION
Who denied him from seeing the Grail's grace?

SECOND PROCESSION
He whom there you bear, its sinful guardian.

The condemnation of Amfortas by the knights is dreadful and extreme. Wagner is trying to make it clear how restrictive religion can be. No wonder Nietzsche and his contemporaries were so against it. However, for Wagner their criticism of religion and their denial of God were just as empty. What is misleading about the knights' words, according to Gurnemanz in the first act, is that the angels never told Titurel to build the sanctuary or to protect the relics. Actually, Gurnemanz said, *"... supremely wondrous wealth of these treasured witnesses ...".* Yes, they were a treasured wealth, but they were *witnesses* of the Divine *Will-to-Redeem*. They were, and are the testimony, the *witness*, of Divine Love. Such a testimony was not to be concealed, but rather revealed. The relics should not be protected from so-called sinners - they should be lavished upon them. The relics were, and are the mediators of salvation, even in Amfortas' present condition. The religion of the knights totally misled the ignorant into believing that such a commission was given to Titurel to protect God. Never!

Amfortas is overtaken by grief that could only be described by music; words cannot adequately color his anguish. He is convinced of his guilt, and considers death a mild penance for his sins. He even asks his father, now deceased, to ask Christ to take his life:

AMFORTAS
My father! As I call to you, I beg you call to Him: "Redeemer, grant my son repose!"

The knights interrupt Amfortas' prayer, once again ignoring the torment of his soul. They shout:

KNIGHTS
(Pressing closer to Amfortas.)

Uncover the Grail! - Serve the Office! Your father exhorts you - You must! You must!

If the guilt of Titurel's death isn't enough, the knights use the memory of Amfortas' father to try to manipulate him to uncover the Grail. They are not compassionate, and they totally disregard his suffering:

AMFORTAS
(Jumping up in wild despair and rushes, throwing himself before the withdrawing the knights)

No! No more! Ha! Already I feel the cloud of darkness of death, and once again I must return to life? Mad ones! Who wants to force me to live? Could you but give me death!

(He tears open his garment!)

Here I am - here is the wound! Here what poisons me, flows my blood. Draw your weapons! Plunge your swords in deep - deep, to the hilt! Up, you heroes! Slay the sinner in his agony, then once more the Grail shall shine clear on you!

Amfortas wanted to die because he was convinced that was the only way he could be free, and that the Grail could shine again. What deception! This is self-flagellation and asceticism to an extreme, and both are nothing more than the *Self-Will* trying to atone for itself. Consider the dichotomy: what is the difference between the two men, Amfortas in sinful remorse begging for death, and Klingsor mutilating himself to prove his worthiness? There is no difference. Titurel's religion prolongs this grim trend amongst his most dedicated followers. It empowers *Self-Will* to permit and even inspires suicide and mutilation.

As the fruit of religion's abject despair reaches its zenith in Wagner's incomparable score, on stage in the darkness, Gurnemanz, Parsifal, and Kundry enter. Parsifal steps forward and extends the Spear toward Amfortas. It is interesting to note another parallelism at this point. In the second act when Kundry was interacting with Parsifal, she called her inner struggle *"madness"*, and called upon Klingsor to strike Parsifal with the stolen Spear. Here Amfortas calls the knights *"mad ones"* and demands that they pierce *him* through with their swords. Nonetheless, the true madness has now arrived! Parsifal - *pure madness* - the *innocent fool - now* enlightened by compassion, will 'pierce/touch' Amfortas' wound with the Holy Spear, bringing healing and restoration:

PARSIFAL
Only one weapon serves: only the Spear that smote you can heal your wound.

(Amfortas' features light up in holy ecstasy; he seems to stagger under overpowering emotion; Gurnemanz supports him.)

Be whole, absolved and atoned! I now will perform your office. O blessed be your suffering, which gave compassion's mighty power and wisdom's purest might to the timorous fool!

(Parsifal steps toward the center, holding the spear above him.)

"PARSIFAL: THE WILL AND REDEMPTION"

The holy spear! - I bring it back to you!

(All gaze in supreme rapture at the lifted Spear to whose point Parsifal raises his eyes and continues joyously.)

O supreme joy of this miracle! This that healed your wound I see pouring with holy blood yearning for that kindred fount which flows and surges within the Grail. No more shall it be hidden: uncover the Grail, open the shrine!

(Parsifal ascends the altar steps, takes the Grail from the shrine already opened by the squires, and falls to his knees before it in silent prayer and contemplation. The Grail gradually glows with a soft light. Increasing darkness below and growing illumination from above.)

With the words, *"... only the Spear that smote you can heal your wound",* once again Wagner merges and adds to existing stories and themes to proclaim his message. The story he used here was that of Telephus and Achilles, mentioned in the Homeric Cycle *Cypria*, and reportedly included in *Telephus*, a lost Euripides play[109]. In one version of the story, on their way to Troy to rescue Helen, the Greeks mistakenly landed in Mysia, whose king was Telephus, son of Hercules. Telephus killed Thersander, son of Polynices while fighting the Greeks. Dionysus assisted the Greeks by causing Telephus to stumble over a vine, whereby he fell upon Achilles spear which wounded him in the thigh, and that wound would not heal. Telephus consulted the oracle of Delphi, and was told that *only he could cure him whom had wounded him.* So, he went to Clytemnestra (wife of Agamemnon, King of the Greeks at the time of the Trojan War) and upon her counsel kidnapped Orestes (her own infant son), and held him as ransom until Achilles agreed to heal the wound. In addition, the Greeks consulted an oracle and were told they could not win the war without the aid of Telephus. Finally, Achilles agreed. He took rust shavings from his spear that wounded

Telephus and placed them into the wound, and it healed.[110] The Greek moral to the story is that, many times we are wounded by those we need in our lives, and as uncomfortable as that may be, we need to return to where those wounds occurred and do what is necessary to restore those relationships, to be healed.

Amfortas was now confronting the real source of his wound. From the religious point of view, Amfortas was full of zeal, and in condemnation and accusation of Klingsor, he went after him. However, his own egoistic pride caused his failure. He ventured where he was not led by the Grail, and when faced with temptation, he was powerless. *He dropped the Spear, it was never wrested from him.* His desire to condemn in the name of religion was why the Spear fell to the ground. His actions were counter to the intrinsic nature of the Spear, the *Will-to-Give-Life*, not the *Will-to-Take-Life*.

When Klingsor threw the Spear at Parsifal, and it hovered over his head, both Klingsor and Amfortas were at the same spiritual level. When Amfortas first pursued Klingsor to destroy him, the Spear fell to the ground because he was trying to use it in a way that was contrary to its nature. Even if his sexual lust caused him to drop it, that lust still also arose from his egoism.

Wagner's message here is that we cannot feed our *Ego*, our *Self-Will*, in isolation, without affecting other aspects of our lives. This is what Parsifal said to Kundry in the last act, *"The solace to end your sorrows comes not from the source from which they flow ..."*. Amfortas could not overcome his lust because it arose from his *Ego*. Therefore Klingsor's flower-maidens were successful; the knights who came their way were on a self-serving religious quest. The squires in Act I say, *"He who brought it back will have fame and fortune"*, revealing their self-centeredness. When the knights arrived in Klingsor's Garden, they were so charged with *Self-Will*, regardless of their pious disguise, that they could not help but fall prey to the lure of the flower-maidens. Their *Self-Will* also fueled Klingsor's egoism and his Enlightenment beliefs. Each time one of the knights fell, it only proved Klingsor's belief that their faith was useless, that there was no God, and that he, through his knowledge of science and nature could be the ruler of his own destiny, and the destiny of others.

The Spear and the Grail function through compassion and from a justice that brings healing and reconciliation. However, when actions performed in the name of religion misuse the Divine — such as judgment, condemnation, and exclusion - Divine veracity is absent. Instead, religion calls for reaping what you sow, or to put it another way, an eye for an eye (i.e., the Biblical *lex talionis*[111]). Thus, the condemnation Titurel and Amfortas used against Klingsor was now turned toward Amfortas. Amfortas used religion and condemned in the name of God, Klingsor did the same by so-called superior reason, without God.

Healing, and by extension, Salvation could now come to Amfortas by his confronting the cause of his wound. The Holy Spear, which was once used by Amfortas to judge and to condemn, in conflict with its true nature and purpose, now was used in concert with its Divine purpose, to pardon and to forgive. Hence, the new paradigm was, healing by bestowing compassion, not by protecting it.

For Amfortas, healing came by surrendering his self-centeredness to atone for himself, and in humility to receive freely-given forgiveness. Thus, Amfortas had to surrender, allowing the Spear once again to be 'at'/'in' his side - the same act, but imbued with spirituality, as dark to light. Klingsor wounded Amfortas with malice and rage; since Amfortas pursued Klingsor with judgment and condemnation. Parsifal on the other hand, healed Amfortas with the Spear, through compassion, mercy and humility.

When Christ was stabbed in the side with the Spear, He received it selflessly, living in the Divine reality called the

Will-to-Redeem. The Spear, the *Will-to-Give*, opened His side and from it, Life, Love, and Compassion flowed - like the male phallus that pierces the Feminine, opening her so blood and water can issue forth in childbirth, giving new Life. Parsifal touches Amfortas with the same Divine Life-Giving compassion. Remember, the Hebrew rendering of 'Eve' (Chavah) is 'Life-Giver'. Amfortas did not have to do religious works or penance; he was simply the recipient of forgiveness through compassion. Amfortas, in allowing himself to be touched with the point of the Spear, surrendered his desire for death in return for Divine Life. Thus, rather than Christ giving him death, as he requested, he now receives forgiveness and the peace to live. Why didn't Christ grant Amfortas death in answer to his prayer? Because death is not within Christ's Divine Nature; in Christ there is no death, only Divine Life.

Wagner believed that all things in the world are connected and integrated. Parsifal brought redemption to Amfortas, and the suffering of Amfortas awakened transformation and enlightenment in Parsifal, for which he was grateful. While not condoning suffering, he acknowledged that it was Amfortas' suffering that awakened the Divine in him. Parsifal's mission then became to sacrifice his own selfish desires for the sake of others, which is *Free-Will-Suffering*. It is not self-flagellation; it is shedding the *Ego* and pouring one's self, like Kundry's oil, into the life of another. Wagner was saying we need to be awakened, but not by reason or logic, because with only reason and logic, we return to eating forbidden fruit, to having a false sense of self. If we only use rationality, that higher path remains closed to us, so Wagner believed. If we only believe because religion mandates it, that higher path is also closed to us. That higher path is only opened when an inner sense is awakened, that is more powerful than the five senses, as if we could perceive with a new, sixth sense.

"PARSIFAL: THE WILL AND REDEMPTION"

Wagner believed that Schopenhauer's world-of-the-*Will* compassionate belief should be reshaped into Divine *Free-Will-Suffering*, and that the Divine and Man were designed to fit together. He believed that we need to recalibrate the senses to see what we could not see before, because the *Ego*, the *Self-Will*, manifested in religion and the Enlightenment, shrouds the Divine.

Parsifal told Amfortas to be absolved and atoned - two powerful words in Christianity. *Absolved* is to be cleared of past guilt, as if one was never guilty. *Atoned* is to be forgiven no matter what one is guilty of. Christ's sacrifice, born of *Free-Will-Suffering*, atoned for Amfortas' failure and absolved him as if he never failed. From a Divine perspective, Amfortas never failed. His religion imparted his guilt, and his memory validated it. Yet when simple, compassionate forgiveness was extended, his *Ego* that was saying *"I must pay the debt ..."*, was crushed. In the end, forgiving himself was more difficult for Amfortas than receiving forgiveness from God. He finally realized that it was his egoism, *Self-Will*, and *Will-to-Survive* that brought about his transgression and made it necessary for him to relinquish that part of himself, or as Wagner put it, *denying the world*. Parsifal then ascended the altar and said, *"No more shall it be hidden: uncover the Grail ..."*. He freed the Grail by uncovering it; Love was no longer shackled!

Until now we have been discussing how Wagner thought that religious dogma conceals the Divine. Parsifal has now removed the dogma and its symbology. There are no longer any prerequisites, requirements, rules, or purification rites to enter the Hall of the Grail; no need for special ultra-holy knights to protect it. Rather, even a common fool can attain the highest summit; the Power of the Grail and the Spear can be experienced by all - the *Will-to-Give* in union with the *Will-to-Receive*, in eternal cycle.

By surrendering selfish desire to the Spear's touch to atone for his sins, Amfortas finally, humbly accepts pardon and forgiveness. Parsifal was enlightened by Kundry's kiss, which in a memorable instant revealed to him why Amfortas suffered, and what caused him to call out to the Redeemer. In that moment he felt what Amfortas and Kundry felt. His cry was not only for himself, but also for Amfortas and Kundry. Parsifal's reconciliation with the Redeemer led to his being a redeemer to Amfortas and Kundry. With *his* kiss, Kundry was enlightened and reconciled, and with the touch of the Spear, Amfortas was enlightened and reconciled. Parsifal had to be awakened first, for all of this to happen.

As Parsifal ascends the altar, he has a prophetic vision of the Spear point issuing blood; which shortly thereafter happens. The stage direction tells us that a beam of light descends upon the Grail as it glows brightly. Then a white dove descends and hovers over Parsifal's head. This is an important moment. In the first act it is sung by youths in the apex of the dome, but there is no stage direction that actually tells us that the dove is present - it is there but we cannot perceive it - it is concealed. By the third act, because of Parsifal's transformations, we no longer need to be told - we are able to see it. In the moment the dove descends, the stage direction is clear, *"From the dome a white dove descends and hovers over Parsifal's head. - Kundry slowly sinks lifeless to the ground in front of Parsifal, her eyes uplifted to him"*.

Why does Kundry fall lifeless with her eyes uplifted? In the first act we described how the Holy Spirit was the Divine Feminine in the original Hebrew, and in the verses that describe the Image and Likeness of God. Wagner is telling us that Kundry and Parsifal have become one; the Divine Feminine and Masculine, the Grail and the Spear, the *Will-to-Receive* and the *Will-to-Give*, have been united. This is not about Kundry dying, but about her uniting with the Divine. Parsifal has become a reflection of the Divine, not in his own self, but through his journey that began with him as a swan flying upward, looking for its mate. The swan which was shot and brought to the 'lower' world by Parsifal in his 'lower' nature, can now ascend to the 'higher' world in union with its feminine counterpart. The parts of Parsifal and Kundry from their 'lower' natures have now been purged during their journey. They first opposing each other, then were tempted to unite egoistically - Kundry whose kiss brought enlightenment to Parsifal, and Parsifal whose kiss brought enlightenment and forgiveness to Kundry through compassion. The two continually interacted, seeking each other in ebb and flow, discovering and revealing the Divine in each other, and finally finding union as one. The Swan found its mate, the Dove.

As Gurnemanz and Amfortas kneel worshipping, Parsifal takes the Grail and offers it to all the knights. While all this is being expressed, there is this final statement sung by all beginning with those in the apex:

>ALL
>Miracle of supreme salvation!
>
>Our Redeemer redeemed.

This final statement - *"our Redeemer redeemed"* - has multi-faceted meaning, with an emphases on Christ Himself. Parsifal, the agent of redemption, has attained absolute enlightenment, and thus, in that respect is redeemed. But more importantly, remember what Parsifal said back in the second act when he said he heard a voice from the Grail, *"The Savior's lament I hear there, the lament, ah! the lamentation from His profaned sanctuary: 'Redeem Me, rescue Me from hands defiled by sin!'"*. Christ, the Savior, lamented - from where? - from His 'profaned' sanctuary. According to Webster's dictionary, not only does profane mean *abuse*, but also *"Not concerned with [religious or spiritual] purpose ..."*[112]. The Savior is requesting Parsifal to redeem Him from a sanctuary that does not concern itself with His purposes.

The Knights of the Grail were religious in the worst sense of the word. In protecting the Grail, they concealed the

Savior from the very people who needed it most. *They shackled love!* By protecting its healing power, they kept it from those who needed it most. By misinterpreting the meaning of holiness, they could not experience what it meant to obtain it. As a result, the knights were deceived into believing that *their* righteousness and superior attainment gave them special access to God.

The Holy Spear was also misused. Instead of issuing the Life Blood of Creation, it was used to condemn and wound - thus, Titurel's sanctuary was violated and profaned. The religion that started with a simple, although misguided idea to protect the relics, the attributes of the Redeemer, became all things but redeeming. Finally now, a miracle of wonder has taken place - the Redeemer has been redeemed. From what? From religion; now all are free to come, receive, and partake of what they need. From the Source of Divine Compassion, all can discover what it means to be absolved, atoned and united with God.

So what did Wagner mean when he said to Levi, *"Perhaps some great changes about to take place in your life ..."*. Wagner's hope and belief was that his Sacred Stage Drama would communicate the Compassion of God for humanity through the *Free-Will-Suffering* of Christ on the Cross. For Wagner, this work, and his previous operatic works, were not intended for mere amusement, or for mockery of race or creed - Christian, Jew, Muslim, or Buddhist. Titurel unknowingly over-protected spirituality with rituals and relics, and with religious zeal that hurt and condemned others. Amfortas in his religious zeal was morally compromised, and suffered personal condemnation and dejection. Kundry struggled with a dual nature, one wanting God, but vacillating back and forth to Egoistic, *Self-Willed*, base natured lusts. Klingsor lost the faith, blamed all things religious, and prided himself on being enlightened, believing that God was dead. Gurnemanz served faithfully, only to find dissatisfaction. Parsifal felt like a fool around the so-called enlightened

"PARSIFAL: THE WILL AND REDEMPTION"

because his reasoning or faith was too simple. All of these Wagner's characters in *Parsifal* evolved, some more and some less, and for many in parallel. Wagner is saying to us that he believed that in Christ all are absolved and atoned, all races, religions and castes, all are welcome to be united with the Divine:

"... this insistent World of the Will is also but a state that vanishes before the One: 'I know that my Redeemer liveth!'"[113]

The curtain falls.

"EXPLORING RICHARD WAGNER'S FINAL TREATISE"

"PARSIFAL: THE WILL AND REDEMPTION"

Walking Down the Green Hill

After the performance and applause, you might join a long cue to wait for a taxi to take you to a restaurant or to your hotel. If you parked your car in the parking lot, it would take you a long time to exit the lot with all the congested traffic. Or, like I have done many times, you can walk down the Green Hill yourself into the small town. Many have taken this journey - sometimes stunned by powerful performance, and sometimes disturbed by aspects of the production. Yet of all the operatic works one can experience, *Parsifal* is one that forces you to contemplate more than just performance and production. You cannot just walk away from *Parsifal* and say, "That was nice". Wagner is demanding more from his observers.

To sit in the Bayreuth Festival House and to experience *Parsifal* in its original home is what the theater was designed for, regardless of how concerning or glorious the production may be. It was first and foremost designed for the mammoth *Ring* Cycle, which was to set the stage for the Sacred Stage Drama, *Parsifal*.

"EXPLORING RICHARD WAGNER'S FINAL TREATISE"

My first experience at Bayreuth was in 2000 and I had the privilege to see a Wolfgang Wagner production with Poul Elming as Parsifal and Linda Watson as Kundry; I was deeply moved. This led me to think of all those who sat in the same seats before me in Wagner's day. When *Parsifal* was first performed, Franz Liszt, Bruckner, Saint-Saens, and Humperdinck were in the audience; one can only wonder what they thought. We know Liszt was an avid friend and fan of Wagner at the time. According to the archives, during the final rehearsal, to which only friends were invited, Liszt sat in the audience, along with Malvida von Meysenberg on one side and Daniela von Bülow on the other. Malvida is recorded as saying, *"I cannot believe the sound I'm hearing"*. Daniela replied, *"I wish I had a mortal enemy, in order to forgive them at this moment!"*.

Mission accomplished! To be moved by compassion to forgive; the consequence of *Free-Will-Suffering* portrayed. It is that simple. However, at the same time, to bring oneself to compassionate forgiveness is what the long, arduous journey is all about. It is about uncovering the reality of our inner, Divine self.

Many people struggle with the life of the messenger, Richard Wagner, rather than exploring the validity of his message. Wagner's message in both *The Ring* and *Parsifal* is not about him being a saint to whom we should give automatic reverence. He was a genius in his art and craft, but he was also a seriously flawed human being, just like the rest of us. That may be the most frustrating and even inflaming challenge we have. Understanding the consciousness and psyche of a genius is not easy. It is like diving into the deep end of a swimming pool, only knowing how to dog paddle. Recently I saw a nine year-old pianist prodigy in a talent competition. He was able to communicate with the average forty year-old at their own level and with their own vocabulary. Then he played Mozart and the audience was equally stunned. When the ballots were tallied, and sadly he

"PARSIFAL: THE WILL AND REDEMPTION"

lost by only a few votes, he still cried like a nine year old. We might just say, "He is still just nine". Many, when it comes to Wagner are so moved by his flawless artistic genius that we expect him to be that same genius in the rest of his life. Others focus on his flaws and have difficulty accepting his genius. Why?

I have been listening to Wagner now for about fifty years. I have walked up and down that Green Hill for fourteen of those years, and even wrote quite a few pages of this book there. I cannot tell you how many people from different parts of the world with whom I have conversed have had similar reactions - totally moved, enthralled, affected deeply, and wanting more. Then someone brings up Wagner's womanizing or worse yet, his anti-Semitism through the lens of Hitler. The two most common reactions are frustration and disappointment, and many times both occur together. Listening to people's serious and sincere concerns, ranging from one extreme to another, it seems that regardless of what point of view one hears, you have to say it is understandable. Once in a while you hear something that makes you feel uneasy, and you don't know why.

Perhaps that is the point of Wagner as a man, and *Parsifal* as his final work. Maybe this discussion is not just about a genius and his flaws, but what a man and his works have to say to us as we try to understand. Perhaps we may never be able to reconcile the apparently disparate elements of his life, but we should try, and then perhaps just accept them.

On the other hand, we do have his writings and compositions. From a psychological point of view, Wagner is known, in both the worlds of leadership development and of psychoanalysis, as an external processor. In other words, Wagner was not one to just sit by himself and contemplate the universe or spirituality and then tell you what he thinks. Rather, for him to process information, he had to talk and write about it - over and over. Hence, his writings were the process, not the conclusion. The problem for us, especially if you read Wagner's writings, is that many times we do not know where the process ends and the final opinion begins. But one thing we can be certain about - when he concluded an opera, *that* was a final statement.

So what is the message of *Parsifal?* It is almost so simple you would not expect it from a genius. Yet as a genius would be expected to do, he takes us on a journey to address every nuance so that his conclusions will be difficult to refute.

Imagine yourself in Bayreuth in 1882. You are sitting in Wagner's living room in Wahnfried after a performance of *Parsifal*. You know Wagner as a thinker. He has deconstructed and reconstructed Kant, Schopenhauer, and many other great minds of his day. He has also done the same for the Old and New Testaments, Greek and Roman philosophy, Norse and Teutonic mythology, and Buddhism. He once had a thriving relationship with his old atheistic friend, Frederick Nietzsche, who if he were in the room with us, would be sitting off to one side shaking his head in disbelief. Someone may have commented that man's greatest achievements to date are in the sciences because they will truly benefit human civilization. After a brief pause Wagner might say:

> *"There is not a truth to which, in our self-seeking and self-interest, we are not ready to shut our eyes even when able to perceive it: herein consists our Civilization. ... Apart from, but almost simultaneously with the outcrop of that torturing of animals in the name of an impossible science ... laid once more open to us men the teaching of primeval wisdom, according to which this same thing breathes in animals that lends us life ourselves .... In the spirit of our unbelieving century, this knowledge may prove our surest guide to a current estimate of a relation to the animals; and perhaps it is on this road alone, that we might again*

"PARSIFAL: THE WILL AND REDEMPTION"

arrive at a real religion, as taught to us by the Redeemer and testify by his example, the religion of true Human Love. ... our whole civilization is going to ground, if not through a lack of Love? ... in our opinion the only thing to lead to this, would be a wise employment of the Schopenhauerian philosophy, whose outcome, to the shame of every earlier philosophic system, is the recognition of a moral meaning of the world; which crown of all Knowledge might then be practically realized through Schopenhauer's Ethics. Only the love that springs from pity, and carries its compassion to the utmost breaking of the self-will, is the redeeming Christian Love ... The blood of the Savior, the issue from his head, his wounds upon the cross, - who would irreverently ask its race, if white or other? Divine we call it, and its source might dimly be approached in what we termed the human species' bond of union, its aptitude for Conscious Suffering. ... The blood of Mankind, as sublimated in that wondrous birth, could never flow in the interest of howsoever favored a single race; no, it shed itself on all the human family, for noblest cleansing of Man's blood from every stain. ... Thus even the influence of our surrounding optic and acoustic atmosphere bore our souls away from the wonted world; and the consciousness of this was evident in our dread at the thought of going back into that world. Yes, 'Parsifal' itself had owed its origin and evolution to escape therefrom! Who can look, his lifetime long, with open eyes and unpent heart upon this world of robbery and murder organized and legalized by lying, deceit and hypocrisy, without being forced to flee from it at times in shuddering disgust?...But him whose calling and his fate have fenced from that, to him the truest likeness of the world itself may well appear the herald of redemption sent us by its inmost soul."[114]

Parsifal can be about many things, depending upon where one is in life when he or she experiences it. But one thing it is surely about is the redemption and transformation of humanity, regardless of race or religion, or of humanistic or atheistic belief. *Parsifal's* intention is to expose and rid humanity of the arrogant - sanctimonious - pompous religion and the condescending - narcissistic - overbearing humanism, where both Titurel and Klingsor abide.

To both religion and humanism, Parsifal, both opera and character are foolish - thus Wagner's reason for calling Parsifal the innocent fool. But again, that's the point. In our complex arrogance we conceal the obvious, which suggests the simple and sublime. From a complex, conflicted 19th Century genius:

"Let us leave Darwinism alone: I believe little can be achieved here on the basis of feeling. Man evidently begins to exist with the entry of lying (cunning, dissimulation) into the powerful series of the development of beings; God will have revealed Himself with the entry of the most unshakable truth into every domain of existence: the way from man to Him is compassion, and its everlasting name is Jesus. ... With the most respectful good wishes, I am ... "

Your obedient servant,
Richard Wagner[115]

"PARSIFAL: THE WILL AND REDEMPTION"

Endnotes

[1] The word 'Divine' will be used throughout this book as a term to encompass the evolution and amalgamation of Wagner's thinking throughout his operas, letters and literary works regarding God, the Holy Spirit, Jesus Christ, the Infinite Creator, the Source of Life and Nature, Nirvana, Limitless Consciousness, Eternal Life, and Spirituality. However, there will be specific instances where we will unpack a particular concept as it relates to Parsifal.
[2] Richard Wagner, <u>Religion and Art</u>, trans. W. Ashton Ellis, (University of Nebraska Press: Bison Books, 1994) 250
[3] Richard Wagner, <u>Religion and Art</u>, trans. W. Ashton Ellis, (University of Nebraska Press: Bison Books, 1994) 213
[4] Richard Wagner, <u>My Life</u>, trans. Andrew Gray (New York: De Capo Press 1992) 5-6
[5] Richard Wagner, <u>My Life</u>, trans. Andrew Gray (New York: De Capo Press 1992) 6
[6] Richard Wagner, <u>Selected Letters of Richard Wagner</u>, trans. Barry Millington, (J.M. Dent & Sons LTD: 1987) 823
[7] By definition it is the clockwise arrangement of successive keys in the order of fifths.

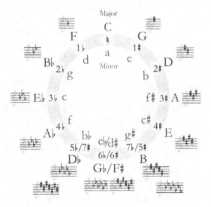

[8] On the lighter side, Meistersinger is a very different telling of the same incarnations and with every intention of merging into a Parsifal-like conclusion. Walther von Stolzing is a reincarnation of Tannhäuser. Rather than the use of rings, swords, horns, spears and castles; Wagner uses poetry, song completions, compositional rules, and of course the contrast of sexual lust and pure love. We must remember that Meistersinger's was first written right after Tannhäuser during the creation of Lohengrin. Tannhäuser fails in the song completion because he violated the sexual purity clause and couldn't win Elizabeth, his counterpart, as his bride. (Once again, the merging of the Masculine and Feminine in the context of the Divine.) Through her sacrificial prayer before God, Tannhäuser is forgiven and the Pope's rod buds miraculously. This all takes place within the context of a Christian setting and God is praised. Both Elizabeth and Tannhäuser are reincarnated as Eva and Walther and where do they meet? In church of course. The story ensues with another song competition this time Walther wins and, like Parsifal, is crowned and is united with his feminine counterpart, Eva. To quickly reference some of these concepts in Wagner's own words, we can look at three key statements. The First is in the famous lamenting aria sung by Hans Sachs, *"Wahn, Wahn Uberall Wahn!"* it's usually translated, *"Madness, madness, everywhere madness"*. But it should be, *"Illusion, Illusion, everywhere illusion"*. According to Wagner he states the following, *"... the curtain rises. Sachs in a chair reading a chronicle of world history ... the low-pitched melody appears ...; to its accompaniment Sachs now begins to sing: 'Illusion, illusion! Everywhere Illusion ...'"* (November 22, 1866). The fact the Wagner tells us he is reading a chronicle of world history suggests to us what the illusion is. Everything that can be seen with the natural eye is where the illusion abides and all things taking place in the quaint town of Nürnberg, are actually universal chronicling. Thus under the large scale grand opera of Meistersinger there is a hidden truth to be discerned. *"It is a wholly astonishing work! The old sketch had little or nothing to offer. Yes, one needs to be in Paradise to know what lies hidden here!"* (December 1861) In Sachs concluding address, usually taken from a very nationalistic point of view, there is another aspect of that seems to make the point as well. HANS SACHS *"Not to your ancestors, however worthy, not to your coat-of-arms, spear, or sword, but to the fact that you are a poet, that a Master has admitted you - to that you owe today your highest happiness. ... Therefore I say to you: honor your German Masters, then you will conjure up good spirits! And if you favor their endeavors, even if the Holy Roman Empire should dissolve in mist, for us there would yet remain holy German Art!"* (Meistersinger, Act III: Scene 5). While Sachs' words have what may appear to be nationalistic overtones, he is not speaking of military might or race as national pride. Rather, he's proclaiming that the poet is the *highest happiness*. Note that when speaking of an Empire, he speaks of the *Holy* Roman Empire, not just Rome as a secular dominating nation. Nor does he speak of German Art, but *holy* German Art. Though it would be almost 15 years before Wagner would pen *Religion and Art*, we see the same concepts emerging. *"If the Holy Roman Empire should dissolve in mist, for there would yet remain holy German Art"*. The Holy Roman Empire spread its Christian gospel by the hand of the sword. Thus, it is 'artificial' and *holy* German Art is 'saving' the spirit of that which is holy. Art saves, not our *coat-of-arms*.

[9] Richard Wagner, <u>Selected Letters of Richard Wagner</u>, trans. Barry Millington, (J.M. Dent & Sons LTD: 1987) 457

[10] Thus Spoke Zarathustra, 1883-1885; The Case for Wagner, 1888; Twilight of the Idols (the title is to mock Wagner's Twilight of the Gods, Götterdämmerung), 1888; Nietzsche Contra Wagner, 1888

[11] Frederick Nietzsche, <u>The Portable Nietzsche</u>, trans. Walter Kaufmann, (New York: Penguin Books) The Anti-Christ, 676

[12] Frederick Nietzsche, <u>The Wagner Operas</u>, by Ernest Newman, (New Jersey: Princeton University Press) 673

[13] Richard Wagner, <u>Religion and Art</u>, trans. W. Ashton Ellis, (University of Nebraska Press: Bison Books, 1994) 213-214

[14] Richard Wagner, <u>Selected Letters of Richard Wagner</u>, trans. Barry Millington, (J.M. Dent & Sons LTD: 1987) 903

"PARSIFAL: THE WILL AND REDEMPTION"

[15] Richard Wagner, Selected Letters of Richard Wagner, trans. Barry Millington, (J.M. Dent & Sons LTD: 1987) 664
[16] Richard Wagner, Selected Letters of Richard Wagner, trans. Barry Millington, (J.M. Dent & Sons LTD: 1987) 895
[17] Richard Wagner, Selected Letters of Richard Wagner, trans. Barry Millington, (J.M. Dent & Sons LTD: 1987) 823
[18] This was in direct response to Nietzsche's statement, *"The founder of Christianity, is as self-evident, without the greatest defects and prejudices ..."* Richard Wagner, Religion and Art, trans. W. Ashton Ellis, (University of Nebraska Press: Bison Books, 1994) footnote 214
[19] Same reference as the previous chapter, *Before the Curtain Rises;* second quote from Wagner.
[20] To Wagner, Brahmanism was the source of Buddhism, *"The two sublimest religions, Brahmanism with its off shoot Buddhism, and Christianity ..."*. Richard Wagner, Religion and Art, trans. W. Ashton Ellis, (University of Nebraska Press: Bison Books, 1994) 225
[21] Richard Wagner, Religion and Art, trans. W. Ashton Ellis, (University of Nebraska Press: Bison Books, 1994) *Hero-dom and Christendom* 281, 283
[22] Richard Wagner, Selected Letters of Richard Wagner, trans. Barry Millington, (J.M. Dent & Sons LTD: 1987) 894
[23] **1.** For Wagner this also is where a good portion of his anti-Semitic views begin. Growing up in Europe in his time, such a point of view was held and grew for over 1300 years. In addition with the advent of Darwinism, this view moved from religious to race as well. In Wagner's day, most believed that if a Jew became a Christian this negative aspect of their lives would be expunged. However, when race came into the picture there is then no way out. You can't be baptized or converted from your race (your blood lineage). Wagner like many others in his day, began to digest this point of view and regurgitate it in their rhetoric. Nevertheless, as we will see, Wagner didn't conclude himself there. Wagner did believe that Christ was so potent that it could cleanse even the most *"deviant of races"*.
2. This dichotomy of the God of the Old Testament and the God of the New, has been a task for the Christian Church for some time. If the reader is interested to exploring this in an in-depth study read, John L. Mastrogiovanni, D.Min., Melchizedek, Our Gracious King-Priesthood in Christ (Los Angeles: Create Space 2013) Available on amazon.com in both paperback and kindle formats.
[24] Richard Wagner, Religion and Art, trans. W. Ashton Ellis, (University of Nebraska Press: Bison Books, 1994) 231
[25] Richard Wagner, Selected Letters of Richard Wagner, trans. Barry Millington, (J.M. Dent & Sons LTD: 1987) 458
[26] (Also known as *Die Nibelungenlied)* Richard Wagner, Selected Letters of Richard Wagner, trans. Barry Millington, (J.M. Dent & Sons LTD: 1987) 745
[27] Michael Baigent, Richard Leigh, and Henry Lincoln, Holy Blood, Holy Grail, (New York: Dell Publishing 1983) 41
[28] King Henry IV in 1804 had the inscription added to it believing that the nail was actually used to impale Jesus to the Cross.
[29] Richard Wagner, Jesus of Nazareth and Other Writings, trans. W. Ashton Ellis, (University of Nebraska Press: Bison Books, 1995) Segment of a letter written in 1869 388-389.
[30] *John* 19:32-35 NKJV
[31] *1 Corinthians* 15:45 NKJV
[32] *Genesis* 2:21-22 NKJV
[33] *Genesis* 1:27 NKJV
[34] *John* 20:11-18 NKJV
[35] John L. Mastrogiovanni, D.Min., The Divine Womb, (Los Angeles: Create Space 2004) 28-29
[36] (A beam of light: the Grail glows at its brightest. From the dome a white dove descends and hovers over Parsifal's head. - Kundry slowly sinks lifeless to the ground in front of Parsifal, her eyes uplifted to him...)

[37] Richard Wagner, Religion and Art, trans. W. Ashton Ellis, (University of Nebraska Press: Bison Books, 1994) Hero-dom and Christendom 279
[38] *Deuteronomy* 23:1 NKJV
[39] *Leviticus* 21:16-21 NKJV
[40] *Acts* 8:26-40 NKJV
[41] *Matthew* 18:8-9 NKJV
[42] In American literature, the tale of *The Ugly Duckling* has been grouped with many of the Mother Goose nursery rhymes and stories. Thus sometimes there is a confusion regarding the origins of the work.
[43] Richard Wagner, Jesus of Nazareth and Other Writings, trans. W. Ashton Ellis, (University of Nebraska Press: Bison Books, 1995) 301
[44] Taken from a lecture on *The Ring*, by the author.

Ring  Transforming the Ring into Valhalla

Valhalla  In the first measure, Wagner removes the forth notes (G# & E) in the Ring motif, which is one full step down. Causing the following note sound the next note in the arppegio. In the second measure, doubles the second notes (G# & E), which was the ones removed in the first.

[45] Robert Beer, The Handbook of Tibetan Buddhist Symbols, (Serindia Publications 2003) 115 *currently out of print.* (There is a reprint by Shambhala Press)
[46] *Genesis* 2:9, 16-17 NKJV
[47] The discussion of Schopenhauer's influence on Wagner can be a very long and controversial. Due to that fact we will not spend a lot of time discussing it, except to say that the background is worth the wealth of information that abides there. A new contribution and recommendation to this discussion is Milton Brenner's, Wagner and Schopenhauer: A Closer Look, (Xlibris LLC 2014) who asserts the connection is overly stated.
[48] You can hear the original Wagner designed instrument that was used at the Parsifal premier in 1882, first in a 1927 Bayreuth recording including the tam-tams and sound barrels conducted by Karl Muck. Then followed by the original instrument played again in present-day (with video). Both the 1927 and present day records are be viewed at http://youtu.be/O89c59k00L8.
[49] Richard Wagner, Religion and Art, trans. W. Ashton Ellis, (University of Nebraska Press: Bison Books, 1994) 217-218
[50] 1 Corinthians 5:17-21; Galatians 3:13-14
[51] Frederick Nietzsche, The Portable Nietzsche, trans. Walter Kaufmann, (New York: Penguin Books) The Anti-Christ, 570
[52] Richard Wagner, Selected Letters of Richard Wagner, trans. Barry Millington, (J.M. Dent & Sons LTD: 1987) 434
[53] *Genesis* 3:5 NKJV
[54] There is an interesting play on words in Genesis chapters two and three. The Hebrew word for tree is עֵץ which comes from עָצָה which means to fasten or close the eyes (see its usage in Proverbs 16:30). To open your eyes to the Tree of the Knowledge of Good and Evil, you shut your eyes to the Tree of Life. You cannot behold both at the same time.
[55] At the conclusion of *Tristan und Isolde*, Wagner makes this same insinuation in Isolde's *Liebestod*, as she passes from this world into the realm beyond. She and Tristan are returning to the Divine Source in the Garden Paradise. More pointedly in the first three Chapters of the Book of *Genesis*, Eve does not receive her name until after the Fall. Prior to that Adam is both the union of male and female. *See Part 2: The Conflict of Reason and Divine Reality.*
[56] Ante-Nicene Fathers, Volume 4 (Fathers of the Third Century - Tertullian)
[57] *Genesis* 3:12 TLB
[58] See the last chapter of this book for comments on this issue.

"PARSIFAL: THE WILL AND REDEMPTION"

[59] *John* 3:16 NKJV
[60] 2 *Thessalonians* 2:3-4 NKJV
[61] 1 *John* 2:18-19 NLT
[62] *Matthew* 14:6-12 NKJV
[63] Richard Wagner, Selected Letters of Richard Wagner, trans. Barry Millington, (J.M. Dent & Sons LTD: 1987) 500
[64] See Act I – Part 2: Religion Threatened by Foolishness, second paragraph.
[65] Richard Wagner, Selected Letters of Richard Wagner, trans. Barry Millington, (J.M. Dent & Sons LTD: 1987) 923-924
[66] Mary Anne Perkins Christendom and European Identity "The Legacy of a Grand Narrative, since 1789", (Berlin: Walter De Gruyter, Inc. 2004) 97
[67] Richard Wagner, Selected Letters of Richard Wagner, trans. Barry Millington, (J.M. Dent & Sons LTD: 1987) 893-894
[68] It is not the intention of the author to discuss the complexities of Wagner's anti-Semitism, except to say toward the end of his life there was some changes in how he approached it. The full article can be read in: Richard Wagner, Religion and Art, trans. W. Ashton Ellis, (University of Nebraska Press: Bison Books, 1994) Quote: Richard Wagner, Selected Letters of Richard Wagner, trans. Barry Millington, (J.M. Dent & Sons LTD: 1987) 906
[69] Richard Wagner, Religion and Art. Translated: W. Ashton Ellis, University of Nebraska Press, Bison Books, 1994; 264-274.
[70] This is reminiscent of Siegfried and Brünnhilde in *Götterdämmerung* Act II, Scene 2, while Siegfried is dying, *"Brünnhilde! holy bride! Awake! Open your eyes! Who sank you again in sleep? Who shackled you in uneasy slumber? Your wakener came and kissed you awake, and again broke the bride's bondage..."*
[71] Parsee is of Zoroastrian decent. The Zoroastrians were the Magi (astrologers) who came to bring the gold, frankincense and myrrh, to the Christ child in the Gospel of Matthew.
[72] Richard Wagner, Selected Letters of Richard Wagner, trans. Barry Millington, (J.M. Dent & Sons LTD: 1987) 877
[73] *Genesis* 5:2 KJV
[74] *Genesis* 2:17 NKJV
[75] Richard Wagner, Selected Letters of Richard Wagner, trans. Barry Millington, (J.M. Dent & Sons LTD: 1987) 664
[76] Richard Wagner, Religion and Art, trans. W. Ashton Ellis, (University of Nebraska Press: Bison Books, 1994) 214-215
[77] Fredrick Nietzsche, Thus Spoke Zarathustra, trans. R. J. Hollingdale (Penguin Press 1969) 44
[78] Oswald Bauer, Wagner in Bayreuth, A Documentary, "I Didn't Think You'd Succeed" (Philips Classics 1992) 66-67
[79] Trevor Ravenscroft, The Spear of Destiny, (Red Wheel/Weisser LLC 1973) 34
[80] Frederick Nietzsche, The Portable Nietzsche, trans. Walter Kaufmann, (New York: Penguin Books) The Anti-Christ, 592-656
[81] Trevor Ravenscroft, The Spear of Destiny, (Red Wheel/Weisser LLC 1973) footnote: 38, taken from *Hitler Speaks: Hermann Rauschning*.
[82] It would be advantageous for the reader to explore Nietzsche's, *Anti-Christ*, for a comprehensive point of view.
[83] Richard Wagner, Religion and Art, trans. W. Ashton Ellis, (University of Nebraska Press: Bison Books, 1994) 230; 244-45
[84] Richard Wagner, Religion and Art, trans. W. Ashton Ellis, (University of Nebraska Press: Bison Books, 1994) 215, 217
[85] Rudolf Von Ems (2014) Encyclopedia Britannica, Ultimate Reference Suite. Chicago: Encyclopedia Britannica.
[86] Jacobo di Voragine, The Golden Legend: Selections, trans. Christopher Stace, (New York: Penguin Books 1999) Saints Barlaam and Josaphat 355
[87] To view an actual picture of the artwork: http://en.wikipedia.org/wiki/Tj%C3%A4ngvide_image_stone

[88] *Matthew* 10:38-39 Amplified
[89] Webster's Dictionary and Thesaurus (Complete Digital Dictionary segment religious 1.) Brackets added by author.
[90] Nietzsche, from *Die fröhliche Wissenschaft (1882)* and *Also sprach Zarathustra (1883-1891)*
[91] *John* 17:21-23 NKJV
[92] *Hebrews* 2:10 ASV
[93] *Luke* 7:44-47 NLT
[94] *1 Samuel* 16:13 NKJV
[95] Richard Wagner, Religion and Art, trans. W. Ashton Ellis, (University of Nebraska Press: Bison Books, 1994) 214-215
[96] "For the earnest expectation of the creation eagerly waits for the revealing of the sons of God. For the creation was subjected to futility, not willingly, but because of Him who subjected it in hope; because the creation itself also will be delivered from the bondage of corruption into the glorious liberty of the children of God. For we know that the whole creation groans and labors with birth pangs together until now." Romans 8:19-23 NKJV
[97] The Five-Precepts or Virtues (known as panca-sikkhapada) the first is to abstain from injuring any form of life. This includes human, animal and damage of nature. (Form more in formation see the Pali Canon, which is available in book form or on the web.)
[98] Irmgard Scharberth, The Evolution of Parsifal (Philips Classics 1981) 5
[99] We use this term here (*anti-Semitism*), hyphenated as is conventionally done, to imply negative attitude or sentiment specifically toward Jews, knowing full well that there are other races who are considered to be Semitic, and recognizing that there is some support for dropping the hyphen and using the term in a one-word form (*antisemitism*). The word *Semitic* was originally coined (in 1781) to refer to a group of languages/races from Northern Africa and what we now refer to as the Middle East - only one (language of which) is Hebrew. The contraction *anti-Semitism* (hyphenated, with an upper-case *S*), first appeared in the English language in about 1893, and although it appears to to be a derogatory term directed toward nearly all Semitic languages/races, at the time it was first used, and now, it has been nearly always been used in an anti-Jewish sense.
[100] Even in a recent Bayreuth exhibit such a claim is made, yet with no clear documentation to substantiate it.

Hermann Levi

Richard Wagner, den Ludwig II. gezwungen hatte, seinen *jüdische* Hofkapellmeister Hermann Levi als Dirigent des *Parsifal* zu verpflichten, hatte diesem nahegelegt, sich taufen zu lassen. Nach Wagners To brauchte Cosima die Hilfe des berühmten Dirigenten zur Rettung der Festspiele. Als das 1888 gelungen war, rückte sie von ihm ab: Das Groß an Levi sei sein individueller „Verdienst", das Schlechte aber gehör „seinem Stamm an". Zunehmend sah sie ihn „dem Dämon seiner Race ausgeliefert: Sie warf ihm „Äusserlichkeit" und „Überzeugungslosig keit" vor und nannte ihn seinen Mitdirigenten gegenüber „die wandeln de Lüge unserer Zustände". Levi war völlig isoliert und bat 1891 um sei ne Entlassung, die ihm Cosima verweigerte. Als die Angriffe zunahmen, trat Levi nach den Festspielen 1894 zurück. Mit dieser Bilanz der zwölf Bayreuther Jahre: „Ich bin Jude [...], so beurtheilt man Alles [...] von diesem Gefühlspunkte aus und findet deshalb auch in Allem, was ich thue und sage, etwas Anstößiges oder zum mindesten Fremdartiges".

Richard Wagner, who had been forced by Ludwig II to engage the "Jewish" conductor Hermann Levi, wanted Levi to be baptized a Christian. After Wagner's death Cosima needed the conductor to save the Festival. Once this had been achieved by 1888 she then dissociated herself from Levi. She described him increasingly as a man at the mercy of "the demon of his race" and called him a "wandering lie". In 1891, fully isolated, Levi requested his dismissal. His request was refused. As the attacks on him mounted, Levi resigned from his post after the Festival in 1894.

"PARSIFAL: THE WILL AND REDEMPTION"

[101] The Genesis Factor Lesson #1 Slide, Copyright 2010

> "...first of all, it appeared an unworthy thing that in the celebration of this most holy feast [Easter] we should follow the practice of the Jews, who have impiously defiled their hands with enormous sin, and are, therefore, deservedly afflicted with blindness of soul. For we have it in our power, if we abandon their custom, to prolong the due observance of this ordinance to future ages, by a truer order, which we have preserved from the very day of the passion until the present time. Let us then have nothing in common with the detestable Jewish crowd; for we have received from our Saviour a different way. ...also that it is most fitting that all should unite in desiring that which sound reason appears to demand, and in avoiding all participation in the perjured conduct of the Jews.
>
> *(325 AD Letter of Constantine to the Churches after the Coucil of Nicaea.)*

[102] "Whereupon Tiberius, who had been informed of the thing by Saturninus, the husband of Fulvia, who desired inquiry might be made about it, ordered all the Jews to be banished out of Rome; at which time the consuls listed four thousand men out of them, and sent them to the island Sardinia; but punished a greater number of them, who were unwilling to become soldiers, on account of keeping the laws of their forefathers. Thus were these Jews banished out of the city by the wickedness of four men." (from Josephus: Antiquities of the Jews, translated by William Whiston, by Biblesoft, Inc., Copyright © 2003, 2006 All rights reserved.)

"It was far other when Tiberius succeeded to the Empire, and Judaea was a province. Merciless harshness characterized the administration of Palestine; while the Emperor himself was bitterly hostile to Judaism and the Jews, and that although, personally, openly careless of all religion. Under his reign the persecution of the Roman Jews occurred, and Palestine suffered almost to the verge of endurance." (from Life and Times of Jesus the Messiah, originally published 1884, Copyright © 1999, 2003, 2006 by Biblesoft, Inc. All rights reserved.)

[103] (from Ante-Nicene Fathers, Volume 3, Copyright © 2003, 2006 by Biblesoft, Inc. All rights reserved.)

[104] The *Genesis* Factor Lesson #1 Slide, Copyright 2010

> "This prohibition [of intermarriage] is to be preserved for the future lest the Jews induce Christian women to share their shameful lives. If they do this they will subject themselves to a sentence of death."
>
> *(339 AD August 13, Law of Constantius)*
>
> "And as for him who begins the building of a synagogue and is not moved by the desire of repairing it, he shall be punished by a fine of fifty pounds gold for his daring. Moreover, if he will have prevailed with his evil teachings over the faith of another, he shall see his wealth confiscated and himself soon subjected to a death sentence."
>
> *(439 AD January 31, Law of Theodosius)*

[105] These concepts are clearly outlined in Wagner's writings, *Modern, What Boots This Knowledge, Know Thy Self* and *Heroism and Christianity*. [See Richard Wagner, Religion and Art, trans. W. Ashton Ellis, (University of Nebraska Press: Bison Books, 1994) 41-50, 253-284]. Also for quick *referenced* writing on this topic, see: Patrick Kavanaugh, The Spiritual Lives of Great Composers, (Tennessee: Sparrow Press 1992) 67-73.

[106] Brother-in-law to Nietzsche; well known for his anti-Semitic views; later founded an anti-Semitic colony in Paraguay which failed; ended his life by suicide following allegations of financial impropriety

[107] Richard Wagner, Selected Letters of Richard Wagner, trans. Barry Millington, (J.M. Dent & Sons LTD: 1987) 914-915

[108] Rudolf Sabor, The Real Wagner (Harper Collins, 1987)
[109] *Telephus* was a lost play of Euripides (c. 438 BC), which included a version of this story.
[110] Ruth Scodel, An Introduction to Greek Tragedy, (Cambridge University Press 2010) 10
[111] *Exodus* 21:24
[112] Webster's Dictionary and Thesaurus (Complete Digital Dictionary segment profane 2.) Brackets added by author.
[113] Richard Wagner, Religion and Art, trans. W. Ashton Ellis, (University of Nebraska Press: Bison Books, 1994) 250
[114] Richard Wagner, Religion and Art, trans. W. Ashton Ellis, (University of Nebraska Press: Bison Books, 1994) 204, 235-236, 259-260, 280, 283
[115] Richard Wagner, segment of letter written to Constantin Franz July 14, 1879. Selected Letters of Richard Wagner, trans. Barry Millington, (J.M. Dent & Sons LTD: 1987) 895

Made in the USA
Coppell, TX
23 January 2024